THIN
PLACES

THIN

ESSAYS FROM IN BETWEEN

PLACES

JORDAN KISNER

FARRAR, STRAUS AND GIROUX | NEW YORK

Farrar, Straus and Giroux
120 Broadway, New York 10271

Some of these essays previously appeared, in different form, in the following
publications: *The American Scholar* ("A Theory of Immortality," under the title
"No Wonder It Quakes"); *The Believer* ("Habitus"); *The Best American Essays 2016*
("Thin Places"); *n+1* ("Thin Places" and "Jesus Raves"); and *The New York Times
Magazine* ("The Other City").

Library of Congress Control Number: 2019953761
ISBN: 978-0-374-27464-1

Designed by Gretchen Achilles

Our books may be purchased in bulk for promotional, educational, or
business use. Please contact your local bookseller or the Macmillan Corporate
and Premium Sales Department at 1-800-221-7945, extension 5442, or by e-mail
at MacmillanSpecialMarkets@macmillan.com.

www.fsgbooks.com
www.twitter.com/fsgbooks • www.facebook.com/fsgbooks

10 9 8 7 6 5 4 3 2 1

Look, I am living
—on what?

—RAINER MARIA RILKE, *Duino Elegies*

I continue to write because I have not yet
heard what I have been listening to.

—MARY RUEFLE

CONTENTS

THIN
PLACES

ATTUNEMENT

When I was twenty I skipped spring break to spend a week in Grand Rapids, Michigan, asking Christians to tell me how they got saved. One of my classes that semester involved creating a piece of documentary theater about the cultural schism between conservative Christians and secular liberals, and it had been decided that one part of the writing team would travel to New York to talk to atheists while others of us would be sent to the Midwest to find the believers. I was sent to the believers.

I spent the week in a rental car with two other students and a professor, shuttling back and forth across strips of highway meeting our interview subjects in coffee shops, motel rooms, and their homes. I spoke with two women who told me Jesus had saved them from suicide, and one whom Jesus had saved from being shot by her boyfriend. We met with a young pastor, vibrant and curly haired, who explained the joy of following a god who instructed you to love people. Toward the end of the week, the professor and I drove at twilight to the home of an evangelical police officer who had moved to the city's outskirts. The house stood, trim and modest, on a wind-chapped block, and the officer let us in his kitchen door as his wife was taking a casserole out of the oven. He was dressed in regular clothes, and he escorted us into the darkening living room, where his daughters sat arranging a puzzle on the carpet. There were two long couches, and we struggled out of our winter coats and settled opposite him to talk. Before I could turn on my recorder, he stopped us.

"First I want to know where you stand with God."

"How do you mean?" I asked, though I knew.

"I want to know what your relationship is with Jesus Christ. Is He your Lord and Savior?"

Maybe everyone remembers themselves at twenty and thinks, Wow, I was impossibly young, but really I was so young, so eager to be good, so doe-like in the face of confrontation. After a brief silence, I managed to say that I didn't know about Jesus Christ, whether he really was the son of God or just a good man, but I supposed his legacy was significant either way.

The man grimaced. "No, that's wrong." He seemed ready for my answer, as if he had been hoping to say what he said next. "Jesus Christ being the literal son of God is the basis of all human morality. It's the truth that our whole lives hinge on."

He went on. "If Jesus didn't die so that I could be forgiven in my brokenness and join God in eternal life"—and here the police officer leaned forward and clasped his fingers together to make the shape of a gun, which he leveled at my forehead—"if

4

Jesus was not the son of God, then there would be nothing to keep me from shooting you in the head right now."

Technically, I have been saved through Jesus Christ. I was eight or maybe nine when a handful of kids delivered my soul to Jesus at summer camp. The twins primarily responsible for the conversion were canary blond, freckled head to toe, and passionate for Christ. The back seat of their mother's car was the site of their first efforts. Camp, which we would attend together, was only a few days away, and they wanted to give me a preview.

Did I know about Jesus?

Did I know He's the son of God, and our Lord and Savior, and God gave Him to us so He could die for our sins and send us all to heaven?

Had I taken Jesus into my heart and made Him master of my life?

Did I know that when I did, the angels would throw a huge party in heaven and then start building my most perfect house there, like, the most amazing house *ever*?

Could I hear Jesus knocking at the door to my heart?

Could I hear Him?

I guessed I did kind of hear the knocking. Jesus was a new fairy tale, walking on water, multiplying fish, but their description of God, an all-knowing, all-loving being who watched over every step I took—this made intuitive sense. I was already aware of a great Somethingness that was at work in the world. The signs were everywhere: the way I saw symphonies of color when I closed my eyes to think; the way ocean tides felt sentient, like a creature to whose moods I submitted my body; the discovery that air looks invisible but a bright light beamed in a dark room reveals millions of particles swirling.

I lived inside what the poet Christian Wiman calls "that universally animate energy, that primal permeability of mind and matter that children both intuit and inhabit . . . that clear and endlessly creative existence that a word like 'faith' can only stain." Christianity offered a new language for that feeling, and, as language does, it reframed my world according to its logic.

My family had never been religious—it was by accident that they sent me to a Bible camp. (The twins had been before, and their mother suggested a group of our school friends go together.) My mother was raised Catholic, but exited the church in her twenties; my father often suggests that organized religion is the world's oldest and most effective smoke screen for human violence, greed, and stupidity. For a brief time when I was in kindergarten, we attended services at a local Presbyterian church at the behest of my mother, but my father eventually refused to go, and so we all gave it up. My brother, so far as I know, has never felt the slightest interest in any of it.

At the camp, which took place in the mountains between Los Angeles and the Mohave, all the counselors took new names in Christ, having been forbidden to tell us their given names, a policy that now strikes me as disconcerting. My counselor, a ruddy-faced and radiant woman who I loved passionately, named herself Sonshine because she wanted the light of the

Son of God to shine through her. At night, around the bonfire, the camp director gave impassioned talks about the goodness of Christ, and asked whether there were any among us who had not yet given our lives to Him.

If today is the day that you want to change everything and be born again in everlasting life, to have all your sins wiped clean and to join with God forever, come down to the fire, he'd say, looking around the little amphitheater.

Kids in sweatshirts with sunburned noses would tramp down the dusty bleachers and approach the director, looking determined and mortified. Counselors palmed their skulls and prayed over them. Some of the converts cried a little, but more often the kids watching did, the ones who had already been saved. At the end of the praying, the counselors would present the saved kids back to us proudly, like gleaming soul-trophies. I declined to be saved in this way, mostly because the spectacle made me shy. Instead, I whispered the "Jesus, I open my heart to you" speech in my sleeping bag one night at bedtime. We were sleeping out on the deck of our cabin, and while my friends exchanged nighttime chatter, I studied the silhouette of the tree line against the stars and repeated the oath as I'd learned it. After, I leaned over to one of the twins and whispered what I'd done.

I'm aware, though I wasn't then, that it's commonly thought that people who go from zero to born-again must be coping with some kind of trauma, or feel broken and in need of saving. That's not universally true, nor, I think, a bad way to find faith, if that's your thing. But as a child, I was neither traumatized nor broken; I was just naturally reverent. There wasn't anything about my life crying out for radical change. I felt, as if on a cellular level, that God was true.

I didn't tell the evangelical police officer the complete truth when he asked, because it had been years since I'd known how to answer his question. People use metaphors like lightning striking or a switch being flipped for a reason—a lot of the time, conversion comes from the outside. It's not so much a chosen reorientation to reality as it is a new awareness of how you have always, blindly, been oriented. It's like Technicolor, the moment in *The Wizard of Oz* when Dorothy opens her front door and the whole familiar world turns from dust and sepia to butter-yellow roads and waxy green leaves and a pond dyed chemical ultramarine and it turns out that the dress she's been wearing was actually blue and there were roses in her cheeks all along, only she didn't know.

With this comes a second, more unsettling, revelation: reality is not what you thought it was. It can, and will, invert—and the moments or spaces of inversion are rarely yours to predict or decide.

Unconversion felt like conversion but sadder, like desaturation to grayscale. The best way I can describe what it felt like is to say that God left. I recognize that this doesn't fit the Christian construct of God—God would never leave because he is always with you, the theology goes, not to mention that there's no corner of creation not "of" God, which means there's no conceivable place for him to leave *to*. But that was the phenomenon as I experienced it: in my twelfth year, or maybe my thirteenth, the feeling of God's presence that had been so immediate just vanished. I didn't know why.

There's a phrase for this in Christian theology: Deus absconditus, the hidden god. Some theologians have framed this as a way of talking about God's inscrutability, the fact that we can't see or hear him, that we have no proof. Others use it as a way of acknowledging that it often feels that God is absent, painfully far away. The playwright Tony Kushner, who isn't a theologian but seems to have read most of them, wrote in his epic *Angels in America* about a god who caught the human itch for new horizons and went off adventuring, actually absconding in the middle of the night. The angels are left bereft and in chaos. "The Aleph Glyph from Which all Words Descend . . . HE Left . . . And did not return." This is more or less what it felt like to me.

I experienced the departure as an exterior and interior silence: I no longer had words for the Somethingness of the world, and so it quietly receded. Of course I prayed. But my prayers and eventually my pleas seemed to fall on deaf ears, and then no ears. By the time I was fifteen, I stopped waiting for it to come back.

One of the features of experiencing the end of a totalizing conviction is that it divides your idea of the world along a binary: There is the world in which what you knew was real, and then the world in which it is not. You belong to both versions and neither. You remold your basic perceptions into a new framework, and if you miss what came before, you rarely say so. You go about the great American work of assigning yourself to other gods: yoga, talk radio, neoatheism, CrossFit, cleanses, football, the academy, the American Dream, Beyoncé. You read articles about the rise of "atheist churches" and notice the uptick in commodified faux-Buddhist principles in the new "wellness industry" and take your SSRIs and try to buy organic.

I'm sort of inclined to say that in this way I forgot about being a Christian for the next ten years, but certain facts make this hard to claim. I pushed for my family to attend a Unitarian Universalist congregation, a creedless, agnostic faith community that, at least in our chapter, declined to refer to God but loved to talk about the interdependent web of all existence. Into my late teens I pored over religious writers like C. S. Lewis and Dante. I took Dante's damnation of the virtuous pagans quite personally. I loved Blaise Pascal's *Pensées*, a series of fragmented notes on the confusion of faith:

> We are wandering in a vast atmosphere, uncertain and directionless, pushed hither and thither. Whenever we think we can cling firmly to a fixed point, it alters and leaves us behind, and if we follow it, it slips from our grasp, slides away in eternal escape. Nothing remains static for us, it is our natural state yet it is the one most in conflict with our inclinations. We burn with desire to find a firm foundation, an unchanging, solid base on which to build a tower rising up to infinity, but the foundation splits and the earth opens up to its depths.

Later in the *Pensées*, he confesses, "The eternal silence of these infinite spaces terrifies me."

In college, I studied religion and did things like spend school breaks asking people who still believed in Jesus to explain to me what that was like. But these were components of a full life that was, at the time, mostly focused on other interests, and I rarely thought directly about my stint as a Christian.

Visiting that church in Grand Rapids was the first time that I had been back inside an evangelical space or spoken with people who reminded me of Sonshine. I felt the impulse to move toward their wholeheartedness, their reverence, their feverish insistence that meaning and goodness and justice had a bigger, more reliable source than puny human feeling. I didn't believe what they were saying, but I half wished I could. It looked nice. Sitting cramped on the couch, staring down the barrel of this policeman's fingers, I understood something already about the stakes, as he saw them, about how people can need to believe in something, and how that need can drive them to wildness.

I didn't think he was actually going to shoot me, though I was aware that he probably had a gun nearby. But I sensed that he believed he would—if the system upon which he built his life and himself turned out to be untrue. I could see in his face how much he believed it.

There was an airless pause as we looked at each other, his hand-gun still pointed between my eyes. His daughters, playing between us, did not look up. After a long moment, satisfied that he'd made his point, he sat back and invited us to begin the interview.

At the end of the documentary theater project, the professor presented each of the students with a book to thank us for our work. She gave me, I think more or less randomly, a paperback copy of *Fear and Trembling*, Søren Kierkegaard's tract on faith and doubt, which I tossed in with the rest of my books and didn't open until years later. *Fear and Trembling* begins with a strange little prelude: Johannes de silentio, Kierkegaard's pseudonym, describes a man who is "not a thinker," but is obsessed with Abraham, particularly the Bible story where God tells Abraham to slaughter his only son, Isaac, and Abraham does it, or would do it. Abraham takes Isaac from their home and rides with him all the way to Mount Moriah, where the sacrifice will take place. Abraham prepares Isaac and raises the knife to kill Isaac, even begins to bring it down, when God commands him to stop, and provides a ram instead.

Johannes de silentio's man wants to understand how anyone could achieve a faith as profound and unshakable as Abraham's, and he thinks that the key is in the story. So, as if he can't think of anything else to do, he tells it over and over. He changes the details slightly each time, as if observing it from new angles. The logic appears to be that circling the story again and again will unlock it, like an incantation. "The older he became, the more frequently his mind reverted to that story," de silentio writes, "his enthusiasm became greater and greater, and yet he was less and less able to understand the story."

I finally picked up *Fear and Trembling* when I was maybe twenty-five and living in New York. I had a lot of free hours to read at the time, and I was in the mood for existentialism—I'd lately experienced one of the radical life upheavals that tend to happen when you're twenty-five. Instead of getting engaged, my boyfriend of five years and I had broken up and moved out, and my future, my home life, my social circle, my reading, my time were up for reinvention. I quit my job and moved uptown and started going to classes with people who worked for hours on a single sentence and talked about devoting themselves to catching inspiration and channeling it into book form. I'd been working a corporate job; now I had a friend who put on a three-piece suit before sitting down at his desk to write, out of respect for the Muse. In a span of eighteen months, my life had grown unrecognizable.

I was happy and I was also burning up with questions, walking around New York, looking for a sign. The world seemed to be made up of a zillion contingencies, impossible if-thens. It was turning out that the all-consumingness of the God feeling I remembered from my childhood was a lot like the falling-in-love feeling, which was suspiciously similar to certain kinds of drug feelings as well as a number of feelings I'd been having about writing. Each was marked by an epiphanic clarity, but every resulting conviction seemed to fall apart. Would this always be true? I waited for the real moment when I'd know what to build a life on and how to be. It didn't come. I looked around:

most people seemed to be waiting, too, though they rarely used terms like "epiphany" or "conviction." I waited some more.

People do the most extraordinary things when they're waiting. In New York, most people do their waiting on the subway, where millions of people at a time huddle together in between where they are and where they want to be. It's sort of hideous, because waiting is frustrating and the subway is gross. The force of so many bodies and their souls in one small place becomes annihilating. People slump and smell and crush up against one another unappealingly, and then they shove and yell to create distance, to preserve the idea that one is not just a body among other bodies but a person, distinct and meaningful. One is overcome with the impulse to say, There is where *you* end and *I* begin, and *I*, in my otherness from *you*, am sovereign. Once, when I did not say hello back, a red-eyed man spat very deliberately so the phlegm landed between my boot tips. This is one way to be in the subway.

There are other ways. If you sit with the oppressive feeling and breathe, you can start to reverse it, to work backward from frustration into a kind of expansiveness, the dissolving feeling of being one meaningful body in a sea of meaningful bodies. Does this sound insane? It is a little insane, maybe. Still, it has its strange rewards. Once, a young man touched my face on the D train. His fingers smelled like cigarettes and they fumbled over my nose and eyelids as he was reaching for something else. I just turned my head some, the way you do when an infant gropes for your open mouth.

When he turned to apologize, he didn't speak but smiled, calm, and touched my shoulder lightly.

"It's okay," I said.

I should confess here that despite moments like this, I am not good at waiting for the subway. I make small, deranged bargains, like *If I walk the length of the platform without stepping on any pavement cracks, it will come.* Anticipation is a kind of helplessness: you can't make the desired or dreaded thing arrive. Whatever you need—to hear back from somebody, to get to work, to get to the hospital, to know how the game ends—is subject to the whims of someone else, or of circumstance or change or, worst of all, time. Time is intractable.

In 2006, the MTA began installing electronic clocks on the subway platforms that informed riders how many minutes they would need to wait for the next train, knowing that people would find this calming. It is calming; it really is easier to wait when someone has guaranteed that a train will eventually come and, better yet, specified its time of arrival. But the clocks also reveal the ultimate immovable obstacle: no matter how badly you need them to, you cannot make the green pixelated minutes tick down any faster.

Even with the clocks, the subway seems to hover outside of time, a "heterotopia," or a space that exists beyond the reach of normal human systems and social mores. Foucault saw heterotopias everywhere: graveyards, hospitals, boats. In heterotopias, certain inviolable binaries "that our institutions and practices have not yet dared to break down" collide and reveal something. In that space of breakdown between, say, "private space and public space, between family space and social space, between cultural space and useful space, between the space of leisure and that of work," he argues, we can look and find "the hidden presence of the sacred."

The subway rarely feels sacred, and yet it is a routine part of my morning commute to observe a woman with waist-length hair lecture the D train loudly about eternal joy and salvation while standing beneath an advertisement for vitamins that reads, "Happiness is simple."

This is an entire subgenus of subway passenger, the one who uses the purgatory of platforms and crowded cars to explain how they were saved, how God reached down from the heavens and pulled them from their own burning pyres and gave them a new life. These people tend to have pamphlets. It seems that most other people on the subways find these people a nuisance—like the mariachi bands or break dancers that rove between cars, but a shade more culpable.

I don't usually care for their specific messages, but I appreciate the acknowledgment that on the average Tuesday morning most people are waiting in more than one way: waiting to get to their stop, but also waiting for news, for inspiration, for intervention, for a promotion, for a diagnosis, for breakfast. The pamphleteers understand that all suspended desire, in some sense, feels the same.

The year I read Kierkegaard, I started spending a lot of time at church, which I told myself was for research but which came to occupy a larger portion of my time than was strictly necessary. It had been accidental, but once I stumbled in, I kept going back.

This tends to happen to ex-believers who find themselves back in church: it's not until you're back in the room, with the faith atomized in the air, the energy rising off the people still inside the system, that you really remember. Call it late-breaking phantom limb syndrome of the soul. The people at this church were lit from behind their eyes. They seemed to be moved by the joy of a single certainty, like a cedar tent pole planted in a field, stillness at the center of swaying silk. As much as I insisted that I was no longer one of them, there was an echo of myself I was remembering by sitting in church, and I needed to stay close to it. My bargain with myself was that I would sit off to the side or in the very back; I wouldn't sing and I wouldn't pray.

I began to feel again the gravity of the Somethingness I had associated with God in my childhood, and with it came a horrible sense of anticipation and longing. All the time my body was telling me that some realization was nearby, some memory, some idea that would change my life. I had also, shortly after beginning graduate school, startled myself by falling in love with a woman, which I'd never done before. I was accustomed to loving and dating men, and so was she, which made it easy for me to shrug off questions about what loving her might mean while we were seeing each other. But when she left me somewhat suddenly after several months, I felt completely, surprisingly unmoored in my own life. I was discovering to my alarm that if I was not religious, I was not not-religious, either. Likewise, though I had never been gay, I was not not-gay, either.

This all happened in a period when everyone kept telling me that I seemed really good. *You seem great*, friends would say over lunch, shaking their heads and looking genuinely pleased for me. *You just seem really grounded and calm and well.*

When I recall this time, I remember an imbalanced attention. I remember high highs and low lows. I stayed out all night with people who scared me. I remember one spring evening, on a second gin when the cherry blossoms were unpeeling in Greenwich Village, everything thrumming so loudly with life that I was seized with the conviction that I was going to die. This must be the body's intuition, an apprehension of disaster; I had cancer, or an aneurysm, or an infection that had just broken the blood-brain barrier. I took the subway home and curled up in bed, certain I was going to be forced to part with everything. I made an appointment for a physical exam; nothing was wrong.

A person who is well does not become convinced she will die because the world is too beautiful. I was poisoned, or maybe clarified, by a pain that overreached its traceable causes. The breakup felt terrible and open-ended to me, besides which I'd had a botched surgery that damaged my tongue and made everything sweet taste bitter, which sounds like a metaphor but was just what was happening in my mouth. These injuries felt like surface-breaking tendrils of the actual problem, which had to do with a larger sense of indeterminacy. I was unreliable, changeful, and as I changed, the world seemed to change around me. I felt sure that there was some certainty just out of reach, or some inbound epiphany, but it never came.

Lots of nights, I'd go over to the apartment of an old friend, a Christian, and we'd make dinner and play music and then sit on his bed until the early morning disagreeing about God. He was a fervent believer, and eager to argue every personal objection I had to evangelical Christian doctrine. At a point, we would change out of our clothes—averting our eyes—and I'd shimmy into his T-shirt and boxer shorts. Then we'd crawl under the covers and he'd read the Bible to me and I'd fall asleep.

It comforted me that he could see that I wasn't all right, and I liked that he seemed so certain about what would fix me, especially since I had no idea what my problem was or what would make it stop. It was a strange, self-consciously chaste relationship. Suffice it to say that after a time he began to actively try to convert me and I began half wishing that his efforts would work.

One night, after church, I broke down and admitted to him that I felt like I was waiting for something I needed. I was exhausted, and for weeks I'd been having the odd, embodied feeling that I might explode. He seemed unsurprised, and suggested I pray about it.

"I can't," I said, ready to weep with frustration. "You know I can't."

"Just go home and try," he said. "Talk to God and see what happens."

I went home. I thought about it for a while. Finally, I lay on my bed and stared at a knobby spot on my ceiling. I lived in the Morningside Heights neighborhood of Manhattan then, and the ceilings were high in my apartment, though the room was dark. The one window looked out at a slant angle onto the fire escape corridor between the 111th Street and 112th Street blocks, and admitted only light that had first bounced off brick.

"Hello," I said to my ceiling.

I suspected there were things about me that were impermissible to the version of God my friend believed in, and knew that there were things about Him that were impermissible to me, and so I was afraid. I didn't want the ceiling to cave in or to hear a voice or to be overtaken by some realization that Jesus was still hiding in some back corner of my heart I'd forgotten about.

"Hello," I said again. And then after a pause: "Um. Please."

People often use the word "ecstasy" when talking about being in the presence of divinity, a word whose root, *ekstasis*, means to stand outside oneself, to be beside oneself, beyond oneself. Lying there, contemplating my knobby ceiling, I was comically inside myself. I thought something might come from outside me and penetrate to my deepest bones, to shoot wisdom into me or wrench a doubt out of me. Swoop in here, I told the ceiling knob, give me something to work with. Please, please call.

No one called. Nothing happened. It was just me, obediently talking to the ceiling.

By the end of Kierkegaard's circling introduction, the narrator is in a state of collapse and rapture. He's told the story all these different ways, and still he doesn't get it. "No one was as great as Abraham," he cries. "Who is able to understand him?" No answer has come. The author's pseudonym suddenly feels significant: "Johannes" derives from the Hebrew Yehohanan, or "God is gracious"; "de silentio" is Latin for "from silence."

It seems right somehow that a book that asks whether a

person can acquire faith just by longing for it proceeds from a failure. Kierkegaard called this section "Attunement," as if telling the story over and over is part of making yourself ready, or as if obsession, frustration, prostration, and surrender are necessary means of "tuning" the person for understanding. Reading the book that follows has a quality of suspense—will he provoke the epiphany he's waiting for by writing about it? He doesn't seem to know, either.

Kierkegaard arrives eventually at the idea that faith is "a gesture made on the strength of the absurd." He calls it the double movement of the soul: infinite resignation followed by a leap into the absurd. Abraham was exceptional not because he was pious but because he accepted the preposterousness of his own predicament—God had promised to make him the father of a nation, but Abraham was a childless old man. He waited for his son anyway. Once he had his much-longed-for child, God told him to kill the child. He resigned himself to the order, taking another leap into the impossible, and waited for it all to turn out okay.

Sometime in the months and years after I lay on my bed talking to the ceiling, I turned my attention away from whatever epiphany I thought I was owed and toward the feeling of standing on the subway platform, the impatience and dumb helplessness and blind trust inherent in this daily exercise. There's a beauty to this state, waiting for whatever, looking for conviction or clinging to it. Assuming the proverbial angels don't come crashing through the ceiling, and they mostly don't, you eventually have to blink a few times, take stock of the fact that you've been talking to a sconce for an hour, get up and go make dinner, set the alarm for the next day. You have to leave the house and continue your commute, join the group, all of us absurd creatures with our wire-and-string certainties forging ahead into our private impossibilities every morning. This is okay. Enough is revealed in the way you wait, and then in the way you leap.

THIN PLACES

The electrode is the width of angel-hair pasta. A surgeon has threaded it through one of the four dime-sized holes in the patient's skull, and it is advancing into her one millimeter at a time, controlled by a small knob that another surgeon is turning and turning with great concentration.

This morning a nurse shaved off the patient's hair, and the surgeon drilled these holes around the crown of her head, two in her temples and two in the back. Then he fastened a metal brace the size of a small dog cage around her head to hold the wires steady as they enter her brain. Surrounding the patient, the brace, and the doctor is a giant O-shaped machine the color of tangerine sherbet, which is taking live images inside her head. The patient is awake.

First, the electrode passes through the part of the brain closest to the bone, the part of her that knows the names of things and left from right. Then it bores down through the part of her that knows how to draw, the part that recognizes her mother's face and remembers what she said to the nurse when he asked about the birthmark on her temple. Down through the part of her that likes sex and the part that knows how to talk. Down almost to the deepest part of the brain, the stem, which is responsible for her breath and her heart. This movement, from outside the patient's body through the opening in her skull and into the core of her brain, is called transversal.

The transversal has been plotted carefully. The path of the wire is precise to the millimeter, avoiding important veins and arteries as well as nerve clusters better left untouched. The destination is Area 24, also known as the ventral anterior cingulate. Hers is suffering from either underdevelopment or hyperactivity, depending on which doctor is explaining it. The electrode will stay inside her to deliver electric currents to Area 24 for the next several years, or possibly forever.

The patient finds herself strapped to a gurney with wide belts, naked under her paper gown, because this morning, like every morning, she thought, 117 times, "I am going to kill a stranger." A pacifist by nature and in her politics, she finds this thought sickening and goes to great lengths to ensure that it doesn't come true. An elaborate protocol has arisen: every time the thought "I am going to kill a stranger" pops into her mind she jerks her head hard and declares silently, "I am a peaceful person, I am a peaceful person, I am a peaceful person." This quells the panic that rises—Is she peaceful? What if she killed someone by accident? What if she flew into a sudden rage? What if she is, at heart, monstrous?—and works like penance: three peaceful thoughts for every murderous one keeps the ba-

lance tipped in the right direction. This becomes more difficult when the thoughts come rapidly. The number of times she
thinks "I am going to kill a stranger" has to be prime or the
thought's power increases, so she'll restart the cycle as many
times as necessary to bring the count to a prime number. A
twenty-minute reprieve is as much as she hopes for in a day.

She has thrown out all her knives, scissors, heavy blunt
objects, needles, and sharp pens. She stopped driving a long
time ago. She never stands near train tracks or close to people
on the sidewalk, just in case something was to come over
her and she pushed someone into traffic. Despite being shy,
she feels compelled to introduce herself to almost everyone
she sees. Once she meets them, they are no longer strangers
and therefore no longer in danger from her. This has become
exhausting—and alarming to the strangers—so a few years
ago she stopped leaving her house altogether. Now she lives in
terror of what she might do to deliverymen.

Over the years, doctors have prescribed nine medications
in various combinations, as well as talk therapy, exposure therapy, cognitive behavioral therapy, and electroconvulsive shock
therapy, all with meager results. Her case is, to use their termi-
nology, "intractable." She had to sign all manner of paperwork
formally acknowledging this, attesting, for example, that she
knows what the word "intractable" means, before she could
find herself in this room with Frankensteinian screws in her
temples, counting the ceiling tiles. She consented to everything
without hesitation.

The first electrode's transversal produces soft, whooshy
noises from the monitor in the corner. These noises are her

brain waves, tracked by the exploratory electrode, which will forge the correct path before the doctor inserts the permanent electrode. His target is two and a half or three millimeters wide. Once he's reached it, he will remove the exploratory electrode and thread in the one that will be wired to a battery pack sewn in under her collarbone. It will pulse electricity into Area 24 at a constant rhythm for several years, until the battery dies and needs to be changed. She has to be awake during the insertion so that she can tell them what it feels like.

The patient is not altogether articulate about what it feels like. She has been strapped down to prevent her from bolting or fighting or trying to tear the metal cage off her head. This is both terrifying and comforting, as the thoughts are coming in inexorable waves now and she is grateful for anything that will help her keep them from coming true.

This is a familiar scene: the afflicted tied down while being ministered to by some credentialed man in a robe carrying an instrument. It used to be books and crucifixes. There used to be prayer and incantation. Now there are only the muted sounds of her brain waves, the rhythmic beeps and clicks of the vitals monitor, and the voice of the doctor as he murmurs to her through her thought torrent. He sounds calm.

The goal is to alter her experience of reality, "with minimal side effects." No one has been able to tell her whether this will work. Only a few dozen people with her condition have undergone this treatment. Most of them experienced some improvement afterward, but the doctors aren't sure why. Hypotheses change constantly, in part because the only way to gather data is to keep doing the procedure. Once it was thought that the electrodes would interrupt looping neural activity. Now, with more clinical experience, doctors suspect that the electrodes might stimulate neural activity rather than interrupt it. Or they might alter the types of information neural pathways can transmit. The doctors also aren't sure exactly which place to stimulate, but the more surgeries they do, the more likely they are to figure out which millimeter-wide targets get the best results. Each new patient is an opportunity to study how this works, and why.

What the doctors do know is what the ventral anterior cingulate does, generally speaking. It houses consciousness, in the existential sense, and emotional pain. It regulates motivation, impulse control, and the anticipation of both delight and catastrophe. Francis Crick proposed it as the center of free will. It's also responsible, in part, for the human capacity for empathy.

There are, naturally, a number of things that could go wrong. Possible but unlikely: hemorrhage, brain damage, stroke, seizure, infection, death. Possible but slightly more likely: memory "problems," trouble speaking, depression, and mania. These latter risks have an aftertaste of irony. The electrode might turn her from a person who speaks compulsively to strangers to a person who cannot speak well at all; it may transform her mind from one reduced to four obsessive thoughts to one hyperexpansive with mania. She wonders what it would be like to go from having one mind to another and then remembers she has already done that.

The doctor in the paper bonnet interrupts this line of thinking to announce that they're ready to begin testing voltages. The electrode has arrived at what they think will be the right place, and now it is time to see what happens to her mind when they turn it on.

She closes her eyes and waits.

This procedure is called deep brain stimulation (DBS). The patient described above is a composite of people I've met, people I've read about, and people whose surgeries I've seen in videos. She is fashioned after the few dozen patients who have undergone DBS to treat severe obsessive-compulsive disorder (OCD), an experimental application now in clinical trials at Mount Sinai Hospital in New York, Brown University, the University of Rochester, and a handful of other medical centers. Her symptoms aren't so much fictional as typical: thousands of people are crippled by fears of hurting others. It is shocking how many have thrown out their knives.

Deep brain stimulation has been used for years to diminish tremors in people with Parkinson's disease, but it's experimental and controversial as a treatment for psychiatric disorders.* Only a few OCD patients have undergone it (roughly two dozen so far in the current, FDA-approved study, and no more than a hundred in the United States in total), and like many historical attempts to alter the mind, it seems halfway magical because no one really understands its mechanisms. Obsessive-compulsive disorder is not like Parkinson's disease—the symp-

---

* Nevertheless, it's being researched with enthusiasm as a possible alternative to the neurosurgical protocol that preceded it, ablation, in which targeted parts of the brain circuitry are burned by lasers until permanently "neutralized." Deep brain stimulation, for all its echoes of dystopian sci-fi, has the advantage of being adjustable and, for the most part, reversible.

toms aren't visible and physical (trembling hands) so much as experiential and behavioral—so neurosurgery-as-treatment becomes more existential in its implications. Compounding this is the fact that, neurochemically, obsessive-compulsive disorder bears a conspicuous resemblance to falling in love. Scientists have scanned the brains of the pathologically obsessive and held them up next to brain scans of the lovestruck, and the images had turned colors in the same places. Doctors drew blood and found the same chemical imbalances. The philosophical distinction between deactivating a part of someone's brain and deactivating some part of their mind or self begins to blur.

I've done months of research about deep brain stimulation—reviewing articles, deciphering studies, interviewing physicians, scrolling through procedure videos on YouTube—for no special reason other than what you might generously call a persistent curiosity. While reading the literature, I find it easy to think in clinical abstractions, but then I watched a video of an older woman undergoing the procedure and was struck by the way her voice was muffled by the nest of equipment. The doctors kept having to ask her to speak up during the adjustment phase, when she was supposed to be reporting changes in her psychological state. "I said I almost just laughed," she repeated, gazing at the equipment before her with an expression of wonder. "I haven't laughed in . . . a very long time." The doctor nodded dispassionately. "Can you describe that for us?"

It seems important to cling to the concrete, to remember that illness is not a metaphor or a study but a phenomenon unfolding in and on real bodies in real rooms. Its qualia, the crinkly paper hospital gown and metallic adrenaline taste, the mutable and inexpressible shades of pain, demand articulation because they matter. We work so hard at telling others *what it is like* to be sick in whichever particular way we are sick; we are reassured to hear that our particulars fit within larger known narratives of illness. With sickness as with anything else, communicating what it is like so others can know, or understanding others in precisely the way they wish we could, is next to impossible. We try anyway.

Admittedly, most OCD patients are not like my imagined girl. Usually, the disease is damaging but not devastating in a relationship-ruining, inpatient-care, life-disintegrating way. It is considered a less challenging diagnosis than, for example, bipolar disorder, schizophrenia, or any of the personality disorders.* It is "neurosis," not "psychosis," "mental illness" as opposed to "insanity." The existence of the DBS study, though, and the interest it draws from patients and practitioners alike subtly undermine this differentiation. Extreme treatment reflects the disease's extreme power to cripple.

Neurologically, OCD and schizophrenia seem to act on similar parts of the brain; experientially, both diseases are marked by foreign-seeming intrusions on the mind. Patients with both disorders are overcome with thoughts, images, and impulses that are, to use the clinical word, ego-dystonic: they

---

* It's worth noting, though, that OCD has something like a 91 percent lifetime co-morbidity with other Axis I diseases, most commonly depression, generalized anxiety disorder, panic disorder, addiction, and anorexia/bulimia. In a study published in 2008, three-quarters of OCD patients from a clinical sample met the criteria for lifetime mood disorders, nearly 40 percent were unable to work because of psychopathologies, and 14 percent were on disability specifically for OCD. In light of these numbers, a diagnosis of OCD is sufficiently grim.

feel alien to and in conflict with the self. They feel other. In obsessive-compulsive patients, these thoughts tend to be violent or violating, obscene, immoral, or otherwise frightening. (The compulsions that result, like hand-washing or counting, may not look very frightening, or like much at all. I know a woman who was obsessed as a teenager with an overwhelming terror that she would die of syphilis; she coped by refusing to say certain words, which almost no one noticed.)

One thing that distinguishes obsessive-compulsive patients from people with schizophrenia is their experience of this paradox: the thoughts hijacking their minds feel urgently not "theirs," but are nevertheless innate to their own minds and bodies. These thoughts feel alien, but not externally imposed. In the medical community, this is known as "insight."

Having insight is not enough to make the thoughts go away. A little while ago, I was talking to a writer who has to touch things—all the banister posts on the staircase, all the poles as he walks down the street. He knows this doesn't make sense. Sometimes, though not terribly often, he has to go back home to confirm that he didn't leave a cigarette burning, even when he can remember perfectly well that he didn't. He has to do this only when alone. When he's with people, he doesn't have to touch anything.

He told me that since childhood he's been fascinated with the idea that everyone is God. I asked him what he meant, and he said that he had a suspicion that God was everywhere and everyone, and all our souls are the same soul, God's soul, but we're just walking around in different meat suits. That's how he said it: "We're all stuck in our own meat suits."

I suddenly felt very aware of how different he and I look—his height and beard and age, his ruddiness, his tie; my stringy arms, bitten nails, and freckles. He is older than I am, and bigger, and embodied in a sort of ragged, robust way that I am not. At first I couldn't quite tell whether he was fucking with me when he leaned in and looked into my brown eyes with his blue ones and said, "What I'm saying is that maybe we're all the same, we just don't know it because we're separated into our own bodies," but then I decided that he was not fucking with me and was serious, at least partly, about this hypothetical.

And part of me was thinking, Get a grip.

Another part was thinking, Well, exactly.

Which did not signal that I was on board with the meat-suit theory per se, only that I was not surprised, even a little, to discover another person with OCD who'd been worrying his whole life about the distinctions and correspondences between himself and other people, and between himself and God. You don't have to have OCD or any mental illness to have concerns like this, but the urgency of locating the boundaries of the self, the distinction between what is inside and outside, you and not-you, becomes particularly acute when your mind seems a little too permeable.

"Obsession" was initially a term of warfare. In Latin, *obsessio* indicated the first phase of a siege on a city, when the city was surrounded on all sides but its citadel remained intact. *Obsessio* was followed by *possessio*, when the attacker breached the walls and took the city from the inside. In *Obsession: A History*, Lennard Davis illuminates the way these two words were adapted to explain demonic possession in the third century: "In the case of obsession, that person was aware of being besieged by the devil since the demon did not have complete control, had not entered the city of the soul, and the victim could therefore attempt to resist." Demonology was, for many centuries thereafter, the only language available for explaining obsession and other insanities. Obsession was understood as a torment of the soul and, often, a spiritual punishment. The cure was exorcism.

This went on for more than a thousand years, until the Protestant church eliminated possession in 1736 (piqued at the way the Catholic Church had, per Davis, "the inside track on exorcisms") and the English Parliament repealed laws banning witchcraft, which had been the most common grounds for exorcism. Modern medicine was in its nascent stages, and as it developed, it annexed mental affliction, recategorizing madness as a physical rather than spiritual problem. The demonological model was replaced by the medical model. Scientists discovered the nervous system and, with it, "nerves," and the possibility of a physiological source of mental states.* Davis notes, "The nerves are the physical link to the mental—they are dissectible, discernable, and physical, yet their effects are metaphysical, symbolic, and affective."

In the same era, the notion of "partial madness" emerged

---

*In the seventeenth and early eighteenth centuries, nerves were thought of primarily as connective tissues in musculature. It wasn't until later in the eighteenth century that the nervous system was understood to have any relationship with emotion. With this switch came the association of the word "nerves" with anxiety, nervousness, hysteria, and other "morbid affections."

to accommodate people who were mentally ill but tethered enough to reality to recognize their illness or sane enough to function within society. One could be "a conscious 'I' who is watching an obsessed self instead of a deranged and unconscious self dwelling in a lunatic." Sanity went from a binary category (sane/insane) to a triad: you could be lucid, a lunatic, or a neurotic.

Among the neurotics, the "monomaniacs," as obsessives came to be known, were the stars of this new formulation. The monomaniac tended to be high functioning and highly thought of. Davis writes, "A certain cachet developed, a notion of being fashionable, in having one of these partial, intermittent conditions." Neurosis was constructed as an affliction, but also a possible asset. It was a sign of advancement, complexity, genius, cosmopolitanism, and, so to speak, *heightened sensibilities*.*

Such was the case with Sigmund Freud's most famous obsessive. The Rat Man, as Freud nicknamed him to protect his identity, was clever and charming, a successful professional man who was nevertheless ruled by disturbing fantasies of rodents attacking his father and fiancée. Freud, writing in 1909, took a therapeutic approach to the Rat Man that became typical for a time: the man's problems were purely issues of the psyche.

---

* The particular metaphors that arose around neurosis, or "nervous diseases," are suspiciously similar to the metaphors that, in *Illness as Metaphor*, Susan Sontag argued were associated with tuberculosis in the nineteenth century: nobility of soul, creativity, Romantic melancholy, et cetera. Sontag was unimpressed with this equation: "My point is that illness is *not* a metaphor," she wrote, "and that the most truthful way of regarding illness—and the healthiest way of being ill—is one most purified of, most resistant to, metaphoric thinking. Yet it is hardly possible to take up one's residence in the kingdom of the ill unprejudiced by the lurid metaphors with which it has been landscaped." Later in the book, she lambasted the modern impulse to psychologize disease, declaring psychology a "sublimated spiritualism."

His obsessions stemmed from the fact that he'd been punished for masturbating as a child, and had been formed as a defense mechanism against the anger, aggression, and anxiety he felt in his adult relationships. The cure: analysis.

A hundred years later, we don't think of the mind as something that can be entered, invaded, or deciphered so much as something that can be altered and adjusted. The mind is less the point, actually—many of Freud's theories and methods are now discredited or passé. "Mental illness" is no longer a breach of the self but a neurochemical event happening to—but separate from—the self. Like hypertension, it happens in our cells, and we swallow pills to get rid of it.

This is more or less how grown-ups talked about what was wrong with me for several years after I was diagnosed with OCD at thirteen. I was, clinically, a nervous wreck, and many of my fears were about the transformation of my own mind. Was I insane? Was I doomed? Was this who I really was? Therapists and my parents were ready with reassurances that what was happening was only an accident of serotonin, a mysterious but correctable "imbalance" no more essential to who I was than a flu or a sunburn. I balked at taking medication, worried it would change something essential about my personality. "You have an illness, and this is just medicine to correct that illness," I was told. "It's like having diabetes. You wouldn't refuse insulin because your body's 'authentic' state is to have diabetes." In the end, I couldn't take the panic attacks, so I took the Prozac and, with it, this narrative of what was happening. It worked. The pills made my hands shake, but my mind was returned back, more or less, to the healthy, stable state I remembered.

When I was seventeen, not long after weaning myself off Prozac, I relapsed. It happened sort of slowly. The thoughts came back, but at first I could fend them off. I blew past them with the buoyancy of a teenager whose life was going well. I was a few months away from leaving for what seemed like the most exciting college in the world, and I had my first boyfriend. Gradually, though, I stopped being able to ignore the thoughts. They came too quickly, and one day they seemed to bring real danger with them. Something darkly magical began to happen: I would gaze out at sunny days, beach days, Southern California sunsets, and feel the sidewalks begin to warp. The sky was cloudless, but something was terribly wrong. This feeling would steal an hour one day, and then I'd be myself again. The next day, two hours. As weeks passed, the sinister entered, and sick fear took over.

At the time, I worked as a barista for a local breakfast-and-lunch place on the beach, pulling espresso and pouring green-tea lattes in an eight-by-eight-foot corner of the restaurant's kitchen. A wall obstructed my view of the line cooks, so I spent my shifts in isolation, handing cup after cup out a window the size of a cereal box to a man named Fernando who ate toast with canned whipped cream for breakfast. I'd be making cappuccinos and humming in my little wall-hole and then suddenly, as if from nowhere, a terrifying sentence would appear in my mind. Then another. Then a dozen. Panic attacks rolled in hourly. I began taping poems to the espresso machine to memorize, figuring that if I had to entertain thoughts that weren't mine I might at least try to make them beautiful. I knew what was happening, but knowledge didn't help. Diagnostic categories, the language of treatment—they weren't enough. My teenage hair started to gray; my hands shook at the machine. I was growing desperate. One afternoon, I stepped into the back alley behind the restaurant, dialed my therapist, and told her that I thought I might not survive.

I was understudying Juliet that summer for a local production of *Romeo and Juliet*, which meant sitting in on rehearsals and learning the lines and blocking. This should have been fun and exciting—and it was some days, particularly when the handsome blue-eyed actor playing Romeo made a point of flirting with me. But most days it felt like something was very, very wrong. People often describe the way your body senses instinctually that you're in the presence of a sociopath or in physical danger. The feeling can be confusing at first, because your body is telling you something that your rational mind doesn't yet know. Why do I feel so unsettled when she's so nice? This party is so fun; why do I feel like I have to get out of here? I spent benign afternoons in rehearsal forcing myself not to bolt from the room. The theater, the restaurant, my bedroom— every place seemed menacing and uncanny. I spent hours in complex, circuitous rationalizations and self-assurances that boiled down to, in endless repetition: "But nothing's wrong, but nothing's wrong, but nothing's wrong."

Of course, something was wrong. The imminent danger was my misfiring sense of imminent danger, the revelation that the stability and habitability of the world can change as the mind changes. Minds are not reliably stable or habitable. They are subject to radical and sometimes horrible transformation. This is a danger of the world that is, as I was discovering, intangible but absolutely real.

Juliet has a monologue in the fourth act, spoken alone in her bedroom as she prepares to take a potion that will plunge her into a sleep so profound she'll appear dead. She and Romeo have agreed that she'll drink this potion, and once she's been mourned and entombed in the family mausoleum, he'll come to wake her and they'll sneak out of Verona under cover of night and begin their life together. She's resolved, even impatient, to go through with the plan and reunite with Romeo, but as she uncorks the vial, a thought occurs to her. "What if it be a poison, which the friar subtly hath minister'd to have me dead?" Fairly quickly she dispenses with this anxiety (the friar is a holy man and a trustworthy friend), but another pops up to fill its place: What if she wakes up before Romeo arrives? What if she suffocates in the tomb? Her nervousness takes on a tinge of panic. What if, worse yet, she wakes too early but does not suffocate, and is left alone in the vault "where, for many hundred years, the bones of all my buried ancestors are packed: where bloody Tybalt lies festering in his shroud?" Then she strikes on the most frightening thought: what if she, surrounded by bodies and smells and "shrieks like mandrakes torn out of the earth, that living mortals, hearing them, run mad," is so overwhelmed that she loses her mind? Will I "madly play with my forefathers' joints," she wonders,

> And pluck the mangled Tybalt from his shroud?
> And, in this rage, with some great kinsman's bone,
> As with a club, dash out my desperate brains?

O, look! Methinks I see my cousin's ghost
Seeking out Romeo—

Quickly she is hallucinating with panic. The loss of her own mind, imagined in the grotesque vision of herself fondling dead bodies in the dark, is made real by her own terror. The figure of Tybalt rises before her to kill Romeo. Desperate to make Tybalt—and the vision—stop, she seizes the potion bottle and, in a gesture that's not a little suicidal, swallows it all. She collapses. End scene.

I dreaded this monologue but I memorized it, made notes on it, even diagrammed it. I was convinced that the young woman playing Juliet, beautiful as she was in the balcony scene, failed to capture this movement from nervousness to wild unhinged fear. But I also hoped I'd never have to perform the scene myself. It felt too close. Acting demands letting go of the self in a way that is usually considered self-destructive or pathological in real life; acting demands that you make way for other selves.

But then there's the trick of coming back, of reconstructing the boundaries between your mind and your character's mind. Sometimes this is hard to do. There are characters you don't want to play because you know they'll be frightening to expand into or difficult to come back from.

That summer, when I was feeling very much like Juliet holding the potion, the therapist would tell me, "Just know that those thoughts aren't you. That's the OCD, it's not you." It was a kind gesture—she was offering me the illness narrative that reigns now, the one that constructs firm boundaries between brain and self, illness and consciousness, self and other.

I clung to that for a while, the notion that the maelstrom happening in my brain was not of me but outside me, happening to me. That there was a tidy line dividing "me" from "disease," and the disease was classifiable as "other." But then it became difficult to tell whether certain thoughts should go in the me box or the disease box—where did "I want to throw a rock through the kitchen window" belong? Eventually I could no longer avoid the fact that mental illness is not like infection; there's no outside invader. And if a disease is produced in your body, in your mind, then what is it if not you?

Recently I found an image of Juliet and the potion, a film still taken from Franco Zeffirelli's 1968 rendition that is famous even though it didn't make the movie's final cut. Juliet is shown in profile, dressed in a beautiful white nightgown with long sleeves draping to her waist. Her dark hair, a little tangled, hangs loose down her back like mine did when I was seventeen. She is kneeling at what appears to be an altar but is in fact the carved headboard of her bed; what seems to be the prayer cushion is her pillow, where Romeo's head lay not long ago. We know she's no longer a virgin, but she looks virginal, like one of the saints offering herself up. Her eyes are closed in fear or love or ecstasy, head tilted back in the light that glows down on her wrists and cheekbones. Her hands are clasped at her mouth in what looks like prayer, but if you look closely you can see the vial at her lips.

In a sense, what keeps an OCD patient rooted in the world of the neurotic rather than the psychotic, what tethers her to a certain agreed-on reality, the adherence to which seems to be our measure of functional sanity, is her healthy sense of the boundaries of her own ego—her ability to toggle complex and contradictory conceptions of self and other, real and not real, rational and irrational. She is obsessed, not possessed. She has insight. Most patients, though, have moments when their grip on me/not-me slips. In the medical community, this is known as magical thinking.

Obsessions often feel like the work of some cruel and sentient force equipped with its own devious logic, showering you with the exact thoughts and images you find most disturbing and devising new monstrosities as you defuse the old ones. Obsession knows you better than you know yourself. It outwits you. For this reason and others, insight is slippery even for diagnosticians. How is it defined, and how much of it is a patient supposed to have? Are lapses in insight allowed? What sort? How many? In his 1996 book, *Theoretical Approaches to Obsessive-Compulsive Disorder*, the clinical psychologist Ian Jakes writes:

> The absence of reported insight cannot distinguish all obsessions from delusions. . . . Further difficulties . . . may be raised by those patients who are classified by some diagnosticians as "partially deluded." These patients are held to have beliefs that would otherwise satisfy the criteria for delusions but do not hold these beliefs with absolute conviction. . . . How, then, are obsessions to be distinguished from partial delusions, and how are those cases of OCD where reported insight is absent to be distinguished from delusions?

Almost twenty-five years later, these categories and definitions are still fluid: in 2013, the *DSM-5* expanded OCD's diagnostic criteria to allow for patients who have only "partial insight" or, within certain parameters, lack insight altogether.

Later, Jakes describes a young woman whose case was typical but challenging theoretically. He gives her only five sentences, but the portrait is complex and, in a way, complete. D.S. was twenty-nine and afraid that she might lose possession of her own thoughts, that they might travel from her head down her arms and escape through her fingertips into the world. She worried that she would leave a trail of ideas and images in her wake, clinging like residue to everything she touched. D.S. knew, for the most part, that this wasn't possible, but sometimes she wasn't sure. Her frontiers, the places where she stopped and everything and everyone else began, seemed changeful and pervious. Jakes calls this phenomenon "ego boundary confusion."

I love this young woman with anxious fingers. I wonder about her—what she looks like, where she is, whether she ever got better. If she is still living, she is fifty-two years old now. Her worries have such poetic overtones; they riff on common fears of contagion, which are often amplified and uncontrollable in patients with OCD. "Our bodies are not our boundaries," writes Eula Biss in *On Immunity*. "Fear of contamination rests on the belief, widespread in our culture as in others, that something can impart its essence to us on contact. We are forever polluted, as we see it, by contact with a pollutant." This notion extends past the physical realm of germ contamination and into metaphor. We worry about the "bad seed," and fear that someone's awful luck, lousy attitude, or even insanity will "rub off" on us.*

At the same time, the things most precious to us often risk—or demand—this kind of contagion. The "sacred" places of the body are the ones where membranes are exposed: our mouths, our eyes, our genitals, the places where we connect with others and make ourselves vulnerable to them.

Accordingly, it is just as common to look for membranes where there are none. We trace our fingers over the faces or bodies of people we love as if we wish we could leave unspoken thoughts and feelings behind. We place our foreheads together and press gently, as if to see whether we can merge that way. We struggle toward each other out of our little meat suits.

Sometimes it works. There is a kind of love where you start to lose track of where you start and stop. It isn't typically sustainable over long periods—it can come and go—but this version of total connection, or total mutual contamination, feels in the moment like the central operating miracle of the universe. Near the end of Toni Morrison's *Beloved*, the prose breaks down in an ecstatic rush:

---

* Two roommates, one family member, and a handful of acquaintances have half joked to me, independently of one another, that they "caught" OCD after watching the television show *Monk*, by which they usually meant that they'd started buying hand sanitizer and color-coding their folders. These are instances of the way we subtly assume mental states can be "catching," but also examples of the way OCD has become equated with desirable perfectionism, much as it was equated with sophistication in the nineteenth century. In certain circles, it is now a form of poorly disguised self-congratulation to profess, in confessional tones, that you are "totally OCD" about your work, your house, your record collection, your eating habits. Like gluten intolerance, it's an ailment that has taken on chic associations, especially to people who don't really have it.

I am Beloved and she is mine. . . . how can I say things that are pictures I am not separate from her there is no place where I stop her face is my own and I want to be there in the place where her face is and to be looking at it too a hot thing

This is an exact description of that love. In the book, though, it is also a description of a furious, sublimated obsession, a daughter haunting the mother who killed her. It's a story about love but, just as important, about horror; a thwarted love so ferocious it manifests and turns its object from memory to flesh. *Beloved* is in one sense a fable about the chiaroscuro of staying half merged with someone else, the redemptive power and the unholy danger of "not separate from."

This is one danger that the current, hyperclinical story of illness seems designed to protect us from. If we are permeable the risks are infinite, and it's comforting to imagine firm borders guarding our soft places. As Biss points out, when it comes to the body, those borders are largely imagined. For the mind, whose boundaries are literally imagined, the notion of borderlessness, of endless susceptibility to mimetic contagion, is overwhelming. But by denying it entirely, by constructing unimpeachable binaries (me/you, mind/brain, illness/self), we create an experience of the world that's soothing but radically impoverished. The other day, I found something in an old notebook that I don't remember writing. At the end of a long list of notes I had given up and scrawled, in big letters, *Where do I start and stop, is what I want to know.*

Sometimes I imagine my fictional girl well again. Out of the hospital, electrodes safely implanted, and responding with promise. Depending on which hospital treated her, she might be sent to an outpatient group therapy called "narrative enhancement."

Dr. Philip Yanos, who developed narrative enhancement therapy, explained to me that its function is to help mentally ill patients overcome internalized stigmas about their conditions. They learn about the ways they have been taught ideas like "I can't have a normal life" or "I'm a bad person" or "There's just something wrong with me." Then they tell the stories of their lives over and over and over to one another. They talk about their lives before they got sick, and they talk about what it was like to be sick, and they talk about now. The therapist and the other patients repeat back to the patient the story she's telling, but suggest more positive language, and then the patient tells the story again but more like the way they said it.

The goal is to help patients integrate their notions of who they were before their sicknesses with who they are now. The task is to go back and find a thread of a story that can be pulled across the hospitalization or the psychotic break or the shock therapy, from then to now, from "her" to "me." It matters what stories you tell yourself about yourself, and in what language. When someone's story about themselves is violated, people get stuck at the point of fracture. They might re-form themselves around the brokenness, or they might restlessly circle forever, trying to understand what broke and why. The importance of the "coherent narrative self" is paramount: without it, even if the symptoms subside, you might never move on, which is another way of saying you might never get well.

This is the story of how my obsessive-compulsive disorder began: When I was in middle school, I had a friend who was going through some major psychological disturbance. She was a new friend, because I was new that year in school, and she revealed her problems to me incrementally, each confession like a gift signifying a deeper level of intimacy. First she showed me the box of safety pins and thumbtacks. She pulled them out of her backpack while we sat knee to knee on the bus and told me that she used them to cut herself. Next she told me she was bulimic and suicidally depressed. Eventually she told me that there was "a thing in her head" named Eiril, and that Eiril wanted her dead. Eiril, I gathered, was something between a voice and a demon. My friend talked about Eiril all the time, as if she were a mutual acquaintance. On days when I'd been a particularly sweet or loyal friend, she would smile at me meaningfully and say, "Eiril really doesn't like you."

We had only a passing resemblance, but still teachers sometimes confused us, and I was quietly pleased at being one of a pair. When she started telling me about thumbtacks and Eiril, I was fascinated and curious and, most of all, thrilled to be brought in. This was interesting and presented an exciting challenge: I would love her to health. She would ask, "Why doesn't it scare you to hear about these things?" and I would tell her blithely, "Because these problems are yours, not mine. You are you, and I am me." This answer seemed to annoy her, and she would change the subject.

One night we were up late talking on the phone while I babysat for the neighbors. *Vertigo*, which I'd never seen, was on TV. In the film, Kim Novak appears to be possessed by a ghost that is driving her to suicide. "There's a woman in my head who wants me dead," she confesses to Jimmy Stewart after trying to hurl herself off a cliff. "She talks to me all the time." Stewart, a sucker for a blonde with a dark streak, falls in love anyway. Unfortunately, he isn't able to love her to health. He takes her to a place she keeps seeing in her nightmares, an old Spanish mission on the coast, hoping to convince her that she can overcome her fears and exorcise the ghost, but she breaks away from him, dashes up the bell tower, and jumps to her death. This moment, at the film's halfway point, marks a shift in focus from her possession to his obsession: her madness transfers to him. Unable to let her go, he is ruined by her.

It was during the bell-tower scene—can this possibly be true? This is how I remember it—as Novak dashed up the steps, that my friend asked me again why I was never frightened by her confessions. I repeated my usual answer—you are you and I am me—and she replied, "You never think you're going to be one of these people, like me, until you are one."

Suddenly something came open inside me, and I knew she was right. I hung up the phone and had my first panic attack.

It's uncanny how closely Novak's confession ("There's a woman in my head who wants me dead. She talks to me all the time") matches my friend's description of Eiril as I remember it, and how closely Eiril and Novak's homicidal ghost resemble each other. The synchronicity unnerves me, particularly because I had 100 percent forgotten Novak's imagined woman until I watched the movie again recently. For fifteen years— years during which I carefully avoided *Vertigo*—I remembered only the bell-tower scene, her gray suit ascending the stairwell and then falling past the stone window.

Did I drastically conflate memories and invent all the details of Eiril in the years since that night? Had my friend seen *Vertigo*, and was it she who suggested I watch it, hoping that I'd see she was not the first person to be visited by an Eiril, perhaps even hoping that I might be visited next—and if so, why? I've been asking myself these questions for a while now. Neither scenario makes sense. I am sure I didn't invent Eiril, and yet the premeditated manipulation required for the second scenario is so extreme I'd rather find it implausible. Any other possibility demands a coincidence on the level of an act of God. This is a fault in this story I can't overlook and can't heal. It just is.

Ever since watching *Vertigo* again, I've been dwelling on the uncanny aspects of this story—but what I've been dwelling on for fifteen years is the story itself. When my friend said, "You could be like me," and I was plunged irreversibly into a new kind of fear—what was that? In so many ways the moment marks a before and an after, but I don't really know how to talk about it. You could say it was ego boundary confusion. You could say it was mimetic contamination. You could say, maybe, that it was the beginning of real empathy. What I will not say is that it was only a chemical reaction, because while that might be correct, it isn't true.

The summer I was seventeen and relapsing, I ran across a moment in the *Phaedrus* when Socrates theorizes that madness "is the channel by which we receive the greatest blessings. . . . So, according to the evidence provided by our ancestors, madness is a nobler thing than sober sense . . . ; madness comes from God, whereas sober sense is merely human." Fuck you, Socrates, I thought.

I have said in my darker moments that I would never wish this mess on anyone, even the girl I got it from. (As if that mattered.) I will probably say this again someday, my whining masquerading as largesse, and I will mean it, but it is also true that I know something I did not know before, which is that we are more expansive than we imagine. And this expansiveness is both powerful and frightening. It can ruin you to madness, or fate or God or disease or demons or whatever you call the unknowables. But it is gorgeous, too. It's how the better unknowables get in. I think about being thirteen and hanging up the phone, standing frozen in the middle of the carpet in the neighbor's living room while Jimmy Stewart watched Kim Novak's body plummet to the terra-cotta and looking at him and looking at her with my friend's voice ringing in my mind and feeling like I was being cracked wide at the sternum and the top of the head at once, being opened and emptied and invaded, aware suddenly of the way poor, monomaniacal Jimmy could be me and strange, possessed

Kim could be me, and my friend with that creature in her head could be me, too.

The warping force of that first panic was truly horrifying. Madness is not some holy blessing; pathology is not the same as pathos. And yet that vertigo has echoes in other rooms and reckonings I've seen, other moments of being opened and emptied and invaded by another person but beautifully, of flinging or being flung wide by radical, magical ego boundary confusions and quiet acts of self-extension over breakfast.

The other morning I heard a woman on the radio describe her art, enormous conceptual installations that involve manipulations of breath and light. As she was explaining her process, this artist used a phrase I'd never heard before: "thin places." It's a Celtic concept, one that stems from an old proverb that says, "Heaven and earth are only three feet apart, but in the thin places that distance is even smaller." In thin places, the folklore goes, the barrier between the physical world and the spiritual world wears thin and becomes porous. Invisible things, like music or love or dead people or God, might become visible there, or if they don't become visible they become so present and tangible that it doesn't matter. Distinctions between you and not-you, real and unreal, worldly and otherworldly, fall away.

The original thin places were wild landscapes because the idea was born in the heaths of Connemara, a place that's so aus-

tere and ancient, so full of twists and hiding places and divots
a thousand years old, that it seems somehow likely you might
poke a hole through to another reality.

But the artist on the radio said that the delight of thin
places was the unpredictability of their location. You can find
them someplace with magic written all over it, like Connemara
or the Himalayas, but they also pop up in dive bars, bedrooms,
hospital rooms. They can appear and disappear.

Because thin places involve an encounter with the ineffable,
they're hard to talk about. You know something has happened,
some dissolution or expansion, but like most things that feel
holy and a little dangerous, it just sounds weird in post-factum
description. It helps to have someone with you there, someone else to feel what's happening so you can look at each other
in awe. Afterward, when you are trying to explain it to other
people and sounding like a New Age goof or genuinely insane,
you can turn to that person and know that it was real. Or you
can choose never to talk about it to anyone else and only sometimes turn to each other and say, What was that? What was
that?

But then, the thin places I've known aren't always places,
per se. Sometimes a thin place appears between people. Sometimes it happens only inside you.

"It could be said, even here, that what remains of the self /
Unwinds into a vanishing light, and thins like dust, and
heads / to a place where knowing and nothing pass into each
other, and through," wrote Mark Strand for his friend Joseph
Brodsky:

What remains of the self unwinds and unwinds, for none
Of the boundaries holds—neither the shapeless one between us,
Nor the one that falls between your body and your voice.

Here, transversal takes on a quality of communion, the kind that arises when frontiers fall—a quality that seems inherent, even in the modern transversals of operating rooms where the new exorcism comes in rubber gloves and medical is miracle and knowing and nothing pass into each other and through. Before the word became the name of a medical technique, it was geometry's nod to the importance of the in-between: a transversal is the line that connects other lines. You use it to discern parallels; taking the transverse of two lines reveals whether they'll eventually touch.

After neurosurgical transversal for OCD, the improvements, if they come, will arrive with time. For patients with movement disorders the new world comes all at once, and the first sign is their hands. As the transversal proceeds, the doctors instruct them to hold out one hand and watch the tremors change. The arms start out waving crazily like hoses left unattended but then, within seconds, shudder to stillness. For the first time in years, the fingers can bend of their own accord to hold a pill or a pen or just to touch lightly. Whatever possessed the muscles is gone, and while it's only electrical impulses, it really does look like a miracle. As a matter of course, the patients weep.

One woman whose name I no longer remember did something extraordinary as she cried. In the recovery room, she sat up immediately without saying a word and extended her new hand to her husband. Improbably, it stayed obediently out-stretched, quivering only a little.

The room went still. The doctors and nurses stopped their work and watched as her husband quietly extended his palm toward hers. The air between them grew warm and vanished, and then everyone was weeping in the fluorescent light.

JESUS RAVES

Five p.m. at the Sloppy Tuna and the Christians are party ready. The house music started bumping around 11:00 a.m.—because it is Saturday in Montauk, and summertime—but five o'clock is the golden hour, when everyone is sun-drunk and loose and beautiful. Girls in cutoff shorts and bikini tops throw their arms around boys in Wayfarers, and sway. The dance floor is jammed and everything is spilling, the effect being that it seems to be raining PBR, and the mixture of sweat and sand and other people's beer feels gritty and warm on the skin. The light slants through the crowd as the sun sets just past the railing that separates the dance floor from the beach, and the visual is stunning: a jungle of skin and light and air thick with energy that is not quite joie de vivre and not quite a collective, ecstatic denial of mortality but something ineffable and in between.

Pastor Parker is standing near the entrance drinking a beer. He's twenty-six and almost aggressively healthy looking. Tawny skin, blue eyes, blond crew cut—he looks like he's straight from the manufacturer, a human prototype intended to indicate the correct proportion of biceps to shoulders.

Next to him is Jessi, also blond, also tawny. Her face is familiar from stock photographs of sun-kissed girls with highlights—wispy hair, round blue eyes, a smile to please—but mysteriously hard to place, as if the lens had tilted. Her chin is soft, not angular; her teeth are slightly crooked. On her wrist she has tattooed the word GRACE, and her right shoulder reads AND THEN SOME because she wants to remember that God will provide everything you need . . . and then some.

Parker and Jessi have managed to locate the girl in the dancing mass who seems most out of control. She's coke thin, maybe heroin thin, and dazed and wild, jumping up and down and waving her stick arms. They're discreet about it—they stand near her group of friends on the dance floor and catch her as she bounces back and forth—and because they don't invite her to church directly, and Parker in his board shorts and sleeveless T-shirt is no one's vision of a pastor, she doesn't realize. If she knew she was speaking to a pastor and his bride-to-be, she might not be screaming into his ear, "I love you so fucking much I'm going to jizz all over your fucking face no really I am Imma come and rub it all over your fucking face."

"You're like my new favorite person," Jessi tells her. "You're like a composite of all our friends. We're gonna be best friends. Give me your number." Cokethin stops running in circles for a minute and does this, and then shouts, "Text me you have to text me right now so I have your number too."

"I am," Jessi says. "I am texting you. You're gonna come out with us tonight and then you're going to spend all day with us tomorrow." Tomorrow, Sunday.

"I'm gonna text you did you text me you have to text me."

"I *already* texted you. I texted you two minutes ago."

Cokethin accepts this challenge. "I texted you an *hour* ago."

"I texted you *yesterday*."

"I texted you years ago."

"I texted you before you were even born! I texted you when you were in your mother's womb!" With this, Jessi wins. Cokethin screams for good measure and then announces, "I'm going now but I'll see you guys later because you're my new best friends kbye," and whirls away off the dance floor and into the road.

They stare after her and then laugh. Satisfied, Jessi leans over and says to Parker, "Now *that's* how you make a Christian."

Parker laughs and shrugs. "Yeah," he says. "In Montauk, that's pretty much how it works."

It was Facebook that delivered me to Liberty Church in 2013. A friend from college posted a video that caught my eye; it looked like a trailer for a Sundance short or a promotional video for a well-funded line of men's accessories. I clicked and was met with sweeping shots of the New York City skyline and two beautiful faces: Paul and Andi. They could be J.Crew models, but they are pastors, and the video was the story of their church, of how they left ministry positions at Hillsong Sydney, one of the most powerful megachurches in the world, and moved to New York, where they knew no one, because God asked them to.

Something about it, maybe the expression on the faces of the people in the video, reminded me of the church I'd seen in Grand Rapids. I closed the video and wrote my friend an email. "Tell me about your church?" He responded immediately, because he is a good friend, and invited me to come check out Liberty for myself, because he is a good evangelical.

I had roughly the same interest in "getting right with God" as in readopting my other pubescent passions—lip gloss, *Rent* the musical—but I tagged along to services the following Sunday anyway. No one seemed to mind when I refused to pray and sat off to the side taking notes. "It's just great that you're here!" they said, and, "Have you eaten? Come grab dinner with us later!"

When Paul and Andi Andrew founded Liberty in New York in 2010, they "planted," or established, not one church but two: Liberty Church TriBeCa, which launched at TriBeCa Cinemas in 2010 and subsequently moved to the Scholastic Center on Broadway; and Liberty Church Union Square, which then met on the third floor of the New York Film Academy and later moved to Union Square Ballroom and then a music venue called SubCulture on Bleecker Street. Even early on, the Andrews planned to have churches spread across the world. This is, for the most part, the evangelical model: constant acquisition of souls, constant efforts to "grow the kingdom of

God." Hillsong, where the Andrews got their start in ministry, boasts more than a hundred thousand weekly attendees at eighty affiliate churches worldwide.

Liberty's church leadership is fond of saying that while each new church they plant will adopt the culture of its local community, they'll all carry "Liberty DNA." What they mean is that each new outcropping should hold some stamp of Liberty's essential nature, its particular way of coming to God. This is a common enough idea within contemporary Evangelicalism because, following the Hillsong model, many churches plant so many outposts that the relation among them becomes sibling-like rather than synecdochic. More broadly, meiosis is the apt metaphor for the last two thousand or so years of development within the Christian church. It's what gave us Catholics, Anglicans, and the zillion kinds of Protestants this world has seen—all progeny of the same scriptural gene.

Attempting to trace the genealogy of even the last 150 years of Christianity in this country—never mind the global church—is a dizzying prospect. From the strict fundamentalism of the early twentieth century to the birth of Liberty Church there have been too many inheritances and rebellions to count. Mutations in identity, politics, and theory multiplied as fundamentalism gave way to the charismatic Pentecostalism that swept glossolalia across the South, inspired a movement of rigorous Christian intellectualism in the Midwest, and spawned hundreds of other subdenominations: congregationalism, neo-Evangelicalism, charismatic restorationism; revivalist communes and Jesus People and Young Life youth ministry; the Confessing Movement; the rise of the Christian right and

Falwell's Moral Majority and Quiverfull; paleo-orthodoxy; the progressive megachurches and the not-so-progressive mega-churches; and the branding-and-marketing-fluent emerging church movement of which Liberty is a part.

Despite all the many branchings, contemporary Evangeli-calism comprises a broad but basically recognizable continuum of inherited doctrine. It was easy to identify Liberty's theol-ogy as more traditional than cutting edge, a near relation to the woodsy California Bible camp where I memorized John 3:16 and prayed for the unbaptized. The pastors at Liberty believe that the journey to both righteous living and eternal salvation begins when you accept Jesus into your heart and "give your life to God." They preach from the Scriptures. They tithe. They consider themselves disciples of Christ, and refer to themselves as warriors for God in a war against Satan, who is not a metaphor but a very real demon intent on destroying each of them personally by, variously, sowing self-destructive thoughts, tempting them to evil, causing illness, and, as I once heard a pastor suggest, encouraging airline representatives to lose their luggage.

They also believe that grace is real, that peace is real, that everyone is deserving of love and forgiveness—and that those things are real because of and through Jesus. They "place His name above cancer." They perform healings and witness to miracles.

The first time I went to Liberty I felt like I'd gotten lost and walked into a rock concert: The house band was blasting anthemic power ballads. There was an iPad on the pulpit. The congregants I met were photojournalists and DJs and brand developers and most of them looked under thirty-five. They drank liquor and went clubbing and took notes during sermons on their phones and Instagrammed the service, which was encouraged; all the pastors were doing it, too.

Evangelicals have been debating for years the extent to which one can be both "in the world" and "of the world." How to balance holiness with worldliness? It's the pastors who primarily define a church's culture, and Liberty's pastors relish the collusion of Christianity and a kind of youth-oriented hypermodernism. Before it was common for non-media companies (much less churches) to market themselves on social media, Liberty was on Facebook, Twitter, Instagram, and Pinterest. Andi wears leopard-print jeans and quotes Kanye in sermons. Her younger brother Parker, who serves as Union Square's community pastor, is a trainer for Equinox. The branding consultant named Steve, who co-pastors TriBeCa with his wife, Rhema, sports the greaser-chic leather jackets and half-pompadour commonly found on British pop music producers. Another pastor, who sports the glossy topknot and punk-polished styling of a downtown gallerist, interrupted the call to tithe to ask the front row if they were into her black nail polish.

"It's adorbs," Parker hollered.

Soon after I first visited Liberty, the church popped up in my Facebook newsfeed again. This time it was a photo of a beach at sunrise: white foam hugging a shoreline that stretched to the horizon, a mirror of slick sand reflecting abundant cloudscapes. The image was warm and dreamy. Underneath, text in a bold sans serif read:

LIBERTY CHURCH MONTAUK

YOU'RE INVITED

JOIN US EVERY SUNDAY BEGINNING MAY 26 FOR . . .

THE WORLD'S FIRST POP-UP CHURCH

Near the bottom, in print so small I had to look twice to see it, there was an asterisk: "DJ will start spinning at 1pm."

I drove up with Emma, a twenty-three-year-old songwriter I'd met through Liberty in the winter. We were introduced at a friend's apartment, and within minutes I decided that she was one of the strangest, most luminous people I'd ever know. She's physically striking—tall and lanky, with long dark hair and jade eyes. There's a glowiness particular to people whose hearts are, to quote Psalms, secure in the Lord, and she's got it. She moves through the world expecting adventure and good-ness and beauty, and mostly the world obliges. She met Ellie Goulding's bass player at a coffee shop and, four hours later, was hanging out with the band backstage at a concert; she gave a ride to a friend and wound up dancing all night with strang-ers in a candlelit barn in the middle of the forest; she struck up a conversation in a hotel lobby and then found herself in a transcontinental courtship with a famous rock star. (First, she asked him if he was a follower of Christ. He was.) This is the type of story she tells when you ask what's up.

At Emma's request, we headed straight to Ruschmeyers, where Parker and Jessi and a few other Liberty congregants were already partying. Ruschmeyers is one of Montauk's scenier nightlife spots, and accordingly is both a breathtaking idyll and a high-octane frat hellscape. The ocean is so close you can see moonlight glint off the water from the bar area, and outside paper lanterns dangle over a wide garden, hung from branches curved to form a leafy ceiling. When we arrived, the air was skin temperature and perfumed by the blooms on the nearby bushes, and young women in microshorts and breezy polyblend blouses stood like stalks around the lamplit lawn in their stilettos.

Inside, gin and tonics were flying. It smelled like college. No one could move because the dance floor was packed to the walls and the only recourse was to simply give up and hump your neighbor. The DJ never played more than a third of a song before cross-fading to another, so Nelly slid into Usher slid into Kanye without ever risking a second of boredom from the dancing throng. In the line outside Emma had been telling me she hates the way modern dating commodifies love. "It turns people into products for consumption. You just try one out, like you'd try out a vendor, until you get bored and then go shopping for another one." The girls ahead of us in line looked surreptitiously over their bare shoulders.

Once we gained entrance, Emma was not two steps onto the dance floor when an enormous linebackerish guy in a collared shirt appeared from nowhere and snatched up her hand, whirling her around and pinning her to his hips. "What's your name," he shouted.

"Emma!" she obliged him, smiling and throwing her arms in the air and swaying in time in a way that was both compliant and neglectful. The music swelled and he took the opportunity to lean in closer and bellow, "WHERE ARE YOU STAYING." Emma smiled the smile of a woman practiced at gentle demurral. "With friends," she answered, and delicately disentangled herself.

The linebacker shrugged and scanned the crowd for another. He didn't have to look long, and neither would Emma, had she been looking. Men appeared hoping to dance, men appeared ready to buy cocktails she would discreetly give away, men appeared and appeared, hungry. We found Jessi and Parker and the rest of the crew smack in the middle of the dance floor, unperturbed by the drinks spilling everywhere. This was their element: a crazy party and, looked at the right way, an opportunity to minister.

This July Friday felt like the summer's apogee, right in the middle of the pop-up's lifespan, which would stretch from Memorial Day to Labor Day. Jessi and Parker worried a little about the ebb and flow of things: the weekend of Jessi's birthday, they had nearly forty people in the Sunday service; other Sundays, attendance dwindled and they redoubled their efforts to reach people on the beach and in bars. Not long ago, Jessi had seen a girl sitting on one of the picnic benches outside Ruschmeyers crying, and went over to sit down next to her. "It was actually this kind of big moment for me personally," Jessi told me. Her voice, high and slightly grainy with a young girl's wide vowels and upward lilt, magnified a little. "Because I'd been doing a lot of questioning about what we were doing out here, and having doubts. And I'd said to God that day, 'Show me You want me here, and I will be obedient.' And I saw this girl sitting on a bench crying and God was like 'There you go.'" Jessi asked what was wrong.

Boy problems. The girl seemed receptive to Jessi's efforts to make sympathetic conversation, but her friends circled, suspicious. Eventually one of them came out and asked the questions: Who are you? Why are you being so nice? "I said, 'I just know that God wants you to be happy. We all go through this stuff, so He just gave me a heart of compassion for you.'" The girls seemed touched; for Jessi, the moment was exactly the victory and confirmation she'd been waiting for.

This particular Friday there was more dancing than ministering. Parker stepped forward into the tight circle of bodies, shuffling and preening good-naturedly. He paused a moment to work the spotlight, waiting for the beat to drop, and crooked a come-here finger at Jessi, who advanced toward him, grinning. He took her hand and spun her slowly until her butt came to rest against his hips. She leaned forward in her maxidress and as the beat dropped, her body hit a ninety-degree angle, her back arching in time so that her backward gyrating met his forward thrusting with a kind of breathtaking symmetry. No one could look away. As the whoops and hollers rose above the music, they began to laugh.

Jessi got saved at four in the morning on St. Patrick's Day 2009. She'd been clubbing. At the time she was clubbing a lot, mostly working as a club promoter, and things were falling apart: a breakup, a crappy apartment, a pervasive sense of hopelessness. "I was doing cocaine and had really bad depression and was taking Xanax and Adderall and all these prescription drugs. I came home and started bawling crying. You know the kind of crying where you can't hold it in? Where you feel like your guts are actually going to come out? It was like that. I felt like I couldn't cry hard enough." She crawled into her bedroom and lay on her bed wailing. Suddenly, though she'd never done this before, she started calling out to God.

"God," she said, "if you exist, I hate you. Why are these the cards that I was dealt? I hate my life. You have to take the pain away." Almost immediately, silence came crashing over her bedroom and the noisy midtown street outside her window. The sirens went quiet and a stillness came into the room. Abruptly, she stopped crying. "I was sitting there and I was trying to make myself cry and nothing would come out. I started laughing. And I just went to sleep."

She woke up the next morning thinking, Well, if God is real and He has relationships with people, then that's all I want. She quit her job, sold all her things, and left on a year-long missionary trip with no plans to return. At the end of the year she accepted a ministry job in Australia and was readying to move when she started having dreams. Every night for more than twenty days she was haunted by vivid dreams about New York. "I was waking up bawling crying and—this sounds really weird—I could feel the pain of the people I was dreaming about. God said to me in a dream, 'Would you go? I came into your room and saved you. Now will you go and save them?'"

First she said, emphatically, no. "I was terrified about coming back. I had found all this joy and hope and I remembered what my life had been like here." But God kept asking, and eventually she said yes. She returned to New York, connected with Liberty Church, and founded FreelyBe, an event planning company that pairs nightlife events with nonprofits that receive a portion of each event's revenue. She started integrating: old life, new life; partying, Christ.

"If you look at Jesus's life, he did missional Christianity," Jessi says. "He went where people were broken. It's so cheesy, but what would Jesus do? I really do feel that Jesus would, like, be hanging out with the homeless in Union Square." She inclined her chin toward me and smiled a little lopsidedly. "I think Jesus would be hanging out in the clubs."

The Liberty kids spent most of Saturday on the beach, listening to the new OneRepublic album and getting tan. When I arrived, they were arranged like bacon strips on the sand. It was like stumbling across a group of extras from *90210*: Jessi, voluptuous and bronze in her bikini; a few of Jessi's friends, bleached blondes with lacquered eyelashes; Emma, with her waist-length hair and constellation freckles; assorted sturdily built boyfriends. Parker padded around in bare feet, aviators, and a muscle tee. "You look like you belong in the Hamptons, Parker," said a girl named Gracie. "You look rich." It was true.

When Emma saw me, she jumped up to give me a hug. "Jordan! I had an epiphany. I want to tell you about it."

I plunked my bag down in the sand and started stripping off layers.

"Last night," she continued, beaming with excitement, "I realized that I think I'm a feminist."

Jessi and Gracie let out groans. "Emma, ew." Jessi shook her head. "You are not a feminist."

Emma laughed, pleased to be shocking.

"What makes you think you're a feminist?" I asked.

"I started thinking about why guys never want to make me their girlfriend," Emma said, excited. "What is it about me that makes guys want to be really good friends with me but not date me? And so I started thinking about, like, the things in men that are universally attractive. The things that everyone wants in a boyfriend, like a guy who will pay for everything, or a guy who wants to take care of you—"

"Wait," I interrupted. "But not all girls want guys to take care of them."

Her face went blank. "What?" said Emma.

"I mean, not *all* girls want that stuff, like a guy who will . . ." I looked around at the others for confirmation, but they looked mystified. Jessi squinted skeptically.

"What do you mean?"

"Well, a lot of girls I know don't even like it when a guy insists on paying for things, and they don't want to be taken care of. They want to . . . take care of themselves . . ."

"Maybe some girls feel that way," Emma suggested diplomatically. "But to me that suggests that maybe they have some other . . . bigger problems with men, you know?

"Anyway, I was thinking about the things that are universally, or"—she nodded deferentially in my direction—"that *basically* everyone finds attractive about men. And then I was thinking about what those qualities are in women, like what are the qualities in a woman that make her attractive to men. And, like, I don't have any of them."

I stared at her. "Qualities like what?"

"Well, I don't have that impulse to nurture or take care of people. I hate cooking, and I don't really care about, like, house stuff. I just want to make art and, like, think about things, and travel and talk to people." She giggled.

At this, Jessi propped herself up on her elbows and shook her head. "But, Emma, God doesn't call on all of us to be the *same*. Imagine how stupid it would be if we were all like perfect domestic homemakers who liked to cook. God calls us to be individuals. You are beautiful and you are wonderful and someone will totally love you just the way you are. Like, just be Emma."

Gracie tipped her head back and hollered, "Let Emma be Emma!"

Parker sauntered over, looking concerned. "Where's the boom box? Did we bring the boom box?"

Jessi rolled over. "Parker, Emma thinks she's a feminist. Will you tell Emma she's not a feminist?"

Parker's eyebrows shot up. "Oh, come on, Emma. I feel like that might be a little extreme."

Another girl added, "I feel like that might be a little *weird*."

There was a pause.

"Does anyone want to come with me to get the boom box?" asked Parker. When no one moved from their towel, he shrugged and plodded away across the sand. The conversation turned to women in the workplace, and Jessi grew emphatic. "It's one of my biggest pet peeves when women say that they feel called to be wives and mothers. I don't think God has ever *just* called a woman to be a wife and mother. That's just biological, it's not a calling." She rolled over to look at Emma and me. "Imagine what would have happened if Andi thought her calling was to be a wife and mother. They never would have planted Liberty, reached all those people. New York would be a different place."

We all sat together quietly for a minute, nodding and contemplating a world in which Andi had stayed a housewife. Jessi, soon to be a pastor's wife like Andi, confessed that she had always told herself she'd never marry a pastor. "I didn't want to be with someone who would expect me to be, I dunno, submissive." She wrapped her hair around her fingers idly. "But then I met him and here I am marrying a pastor. He's not like that at all." It was agreed that it's hard on men when their wives are more successful, or for Christians, more anointed, and that Jessi was lucky to have found an exception.

The afternoon passed the way beach afternoons do: there was jumping in the waves and screaming; there were lamentations at the fact that the guy handing out coconut water in the parking lot had only the mocha kind. The plan had been to barbecue, but by four o'clock the burgers were still frozen and wouldn't grill up right, so Parker dumped the scalding coals in the sand and the group prepared to scatter. Everyone was tired and hungry and sandy and thirsty, but agreed to hit up the Sloppy Tuna for a drink or two, "make some friends," and then go home to shower and regroup before the night-time round.

"We haven't done much outreach this weekend," observed Gracie.

"I know," Jessi said, frowning. "We haven't handed out any flyers or anything."

We lugged the cooler and the grill back across the sand and stood around awhile in the parking lot, checking our phones and waiting for the truck that was coming to ferry everything back to the hotel. Eventually, Emma and I decided to take refuge in the air conditioning of a coffee shop on the corner.

Inside, we sat and sighed, brushing sand off. Emma pushed her bangs off her forehead. This thing with the rock star was bothering her. She wasn't sure it was going anywhere, though she wished it would. "I was praying about it and I just realized, maybe I'm looking at this thing with this guy on entirely the wrong scale. We're so used to thinking about relationships in terms of whether or not our desires can be fulfilled. But there's just a much bigger plan at work. Maybe I can't see our purpose for each other because I'm fixated on my own idea of how it's supposed to be. That's such a narrow way to think about love."

She sighed. "It would be easier except I have Eros for him."

Every single time I explained to a local what I was doing in Montauk, the word "cult" came up. The girl working in a local boutique used it, unprompted ("Well, all religions are kinda cultish, right?"), as did the pool cleaner with sun-bleached hair

I spoke to ("Sounds like a cult"), and the photographer I met at a party sponsored by PBR. It happened somewhere between a half-dozen and a dozen times, which led me to believe that if there was a trick for delivering Liberty's elevator pitch without inspiring suspicion, I didn't have it.

The morning after Ruschmeyers, bleary-eyed, I tried to neatly sum things up for my host, a friend of a friend in her fifties who'd been living in Montauk since childhood. She was incredulous. "They were drinking? And dancing like that?" She wanted to know: "And they're *real* Christians?"

Her son Tyler, a good-natured surf pro in his mid-twenties, sat in a deck chair listening, slowly munching a cookie. He laughed and shook his head. "These people sound like shape-shifters."

I didn't know what to say. Underneath his comment lay a set of premises: You can't dance dirty and have a clean soul. You can't drink scotch and communion wine. You can't love to party and love God. Or: you can't do these things without being either a hypocrite or a predator. It makes sense. A pastor who plays beer pong sounds like an oxymoron.

But around Liberty people, categories like sacred and profane begin to feel fluid, unstable. They're nimble with philosophical ambiguity. "There is a tension in truth," one pastor told her congregants. "We have to swing to one side and then to the other."

Emma pointed toward a line in Paul's letter to the Ephesians: *All things are permissible for me, but not all things are profitable.* "I think the human tendency is to label things as inherently evil or unchristian, but they're not, you know? Aristotle said that virtue is a balance between two vices. I really do believe that God uses everything and anything that is fully submitted to him." By this logic, Twitter and clubbing could be tools of salvation.

At Liberty's regular services in the city, the sermon always ends the same way: the call for souls. The congregation closes their eyes while the pastors speak to the unsaved. They address themselves to anyone new to Liberty or new to Christianity, anyone who may have walked away from religion, or anyone hurting and desperate to change his life. And to those people they offer an opportunity: to get right with God, to give their lives to him *right then*. This is, the pastor says, the biggest decision of your entire life, the passage to new life and eternal life, and all you need to do is raise your hands. Come on, the pastor says, just raise your hands right where you're sitting.

All over the room, members of Liberty's operations team—members of the church who keep track of how many souls Liberty gets—watch closely over all the bowed heads. As the hands raise, hesitantly, one after the other, the ops team scans the crowd and tracks them, shooting arms into the air and pointing to the converter in a silent shout: There's one. There's another. They look around at one another urgently, catching souls, counting and recording as a group who, and how many.

There are hands going up all over the room, the pastor says, and it is so good. Come on, put your hands up. Now we're going to pray together, and as you pray this, Jesus Christ is coming to live inside your heart. You are connected to God after you pray this prayer, and it all changes.

The hands come down and, one phrase at a time, the pastor feeds the words to the assembled:

Lord God, tonight, I give my life to you.

I believe that Jesus Christ died on the cross and rose again in my place so that I could have everlasting life.

Tonight I say I want to be a Christian, a follower of Jesus Christ, placed in community and flourishing.

In Jesus's name:

Amen.

And then they open their eyes.

The leopard print jeans that Andi is wearing have everything to do with this moment. So does the iPad glowing on the pulpit, and the fonts on the projector overhead and the choice of a venue with an enormous shiny bar in the lounge area. Because if Liberty's success, both worldly and otherworldly, rests on its ability to deliver people to God, to "grow His kingdom," then its most important task is to become the kind of club that people want to join.

This is also why the pastors refuse to talk politics with any specificity. When asked by another journalist about gay marriage, Paul replied that he wants Liberty to be known for what it's for, not against. Rhema told a congregation, "Doctrine is not a point of unity, and no one will ever have perfect theology. I don't come to church because we agree on every single issue. I come to church because we are family." I asked a member of Liberty's house band if it was really possible that a church that believes in healings and premarital abstinence has no agenda about abortion or contraception or homosexuality. He suggested gently that I was missing the point. "To be fair, I don't know," he said. "But I do know that the only person never welcome to come to Liberty is someone who is physically dangerous," he told me. "That's the only kind of person not allowed in the building."

It's all so likable. A church designed to make people feel comfortable, included, and inspired. A church that wants to demonstrate at every turn that following Jesus will expand your life, not restrict it. Come on, they say. Just raise your hand. Believer or not, there's something deep-down-in-your-bones compelling about a religious community that dances before the Lord. That acknowledges the wildness of what it's asking you to believe with the response "I know! Isn't it the most insane, miraculous thing you've ever heard!? *Let us be in awe.*"

I had a friend once who underwent a dramatic and—to me—baffling religious conversion the year we turned twenty-one. He'd grown up half-Jewish and not religious, a stoner jazz musician, but one August he came back from summer vacation newly and deeply devout. In a matter of months he acquired a yarmulke and tzitzit, began keeping strictly kosher, and withdrew from what had been his social and musical life. He started hanging around at the local Chabad house. Even his voice began to sound different.

We'd had a close, tumultuous friendship, and his conversion was bewildering for both of us. It also imposed an expiration date: if he hewed to conservative Jewish imperatives about male-female interaction, he'd be unable to spend time alone with me, or hug me hello or touch me at all. The door was closing. For several months leading up to that moment, he would come to my room in the evenings bearing one or another kosher dessert and try to explain what was happening to him. Sometimes he wanted to talk about theology, like the role of sex in a Jewish marriage, or why conversion was completely irrelevant to Judaism. ("You are either one of God's chosen people or you are not. There's no use in trying to be one if you're not, or in trying to reject it if you are.") Sometimes he wanted to talk about what he was leaving behind.

These conversations were lonely, a series of loving but hopeless attempts to map a barrier we couldn't see and wouldn't overcome. There were flashes, though, of the old intimacy. One night he arrived with honey cake wrapped in brown paper napkins and settled on my floor. He rested his back against the door, and confessed that he was feeling conflicted. Soon he would have to choose between the two communities and philosophies of Judaism that he'd become involved with: Chabad and conservative orthodoxy. The orthodoxy, he explained, was a little more intellectual, more theologically rigorous. It felt to him, for whatever reason, like the more legitimate choice, the serious choice. But Chabad had joy, zeal, spirit. He felt like he *should* join the orthodoxy, but he looked at me with pleading eyes and said, "But at Chabad, Jordan, they dance. They dance."

That was the last thing he ever said to me that I truly, instinctively understood.

In Montauk, Sunday morning came mild and hazy. At the secluded beach a half mile from the bar where Liberty's service would take place, there was a minor miracle at around half past ten: the sky broke without ever darkening, yielding fat droplets that seemed to come down one at a time in the sunshine. The shoreline was deserted, and when the rain stopped again the sun kept shining, no evidence but a gloss on the stones that anything had happened.

Church was slated for 11:00 a.m., but when I arrived at 10:40, the bar—named, rather baptismally, WashOut—was empty. Plastic cups littered the tables and the ground, abandoned the night before. An empty pizza box sat partly open near the door. Outside, an aboveground swimming pool draped in PBR flags incubated in the sunshine, beer mixed with rainwater in puddles on the bar, and melted daiquiri abandoned mid-stir in the spinner turned to hard candy.

I picked my way through the back deck looking for a clean, dry place to sit. As I assessed a barstool, a black sedan with tinted windows drove up. The driver rolled down his window and called across the parking lot, "Are you all open?"

"I don't work here."

"Oh." We considered each other for a moment.

"They don't look open," I offered, squinting at the back window, trying to discern the passenger sitting there. "But there's about to be a church here."

The driver thought he'd heard me wrong. I confirmed that this morning WashOut was a house of God, and he conferred briefly with his fare. They sped away.

Parker, Jessi, Emma, and a few others arrived in a shiny black Escalade a few minutes before eleven and began arranging chairs and pulling water from the bar tap into plastic cups for the visitors. They seemed subdued but composed, clutching coffees and freshly showered. Jessi was wearing glasses for the first time all weekend; Parker looked tired but clean and calm in flip-flops and a wrinkle-free chambray shirt.

Cokethin was a no-show. Actually, very few visitors arrived to claim their waters: only a midwestern couple on vacation and a local woman whose enthusiasm for the pop-up caught everyone off guard with its intensity. "I've been praying for you," she confided, opening her eyes wide. "I'm just hoping and praying for a revival in Montauk because the devil has really taken hold here. It's gotten bad in the last few years."

Parker nodded, his eyes straying to the pile of individually wrapped Rice Krispies Treats Jessi was laying out on the welcome table. "Well, yeah. It's been hard planting here. It's hard ground."

She seized on this. "Well, the devil doesn't want you here. He wants to *kill and destroy* you. And me and everyone else."

Three people represented Liberty Montauk's smallest crop yet, but if Parker and Jessi were disappointed, they didn't show it. Parker talked cheerfully about wanting to do Saturday-night bonfires next summer, maybe services on the beach. And on the horizon, more pop-ups: spring break in Florida.

But there were beginnings here. Parker's housemates in Montauk, for example, were "basically all Christians now."

"How many is that?"

"Four, since the beginning of summer," Jessi said, and I turned to Parker.

"So that's four guys in seven weeks who are Christians now?"

Parker's head listed slowly to the left, the words appearing to stall in his mouth. "They're all starting to discover their faith," he said diplomatically.

Once they determined that no one else was coming, everyone shuffled around and sat down in the two rows of wooden chairs Emma had arranged. Jessi opened with a prayer, quoting Matthew 18:20: *Where two or more are gathered in my name, there am I with them.* "You call us to be light in the dark places, Lord God," she added, "and we know you have such a heart for Montauk."

After thanking her, Parker settled himself on a stool, hooked one flip-flopped foot behind a rung, and took a breath. "A while ago, I had a job transporting kids that were addicted to drugs to rehab," he said. "We used to wake them up at like three in the morning and be like, 'Surprise! You're going to rehab.' I didn't stay at that job very long because I got a knife pulled on me, and a gun one time, but actually I really liked the car rides with those kids. I'd talk to them all night."

He told us he'd been thinking about that job since he got to Montauk. Watching the way that the visiting summer crowd partied, the way they drank and used drugs and hooked up, reminded him of something he realized on those car trips. "The deepest human desire is to be known completely and also loved. What people display, the partying, the craziness, is not the problem. It's a symptom. The problem is that they feel they aren't loved." A few people nodded. "That's good," Emma encouraged him softly.

He spoke without notes, but in his hand he held a Bible, the one his mother had given him to carry as he shuttled the addicted teens. He flipped it open to 1 Corinthians 13 and read aloud:

> If I have the gift of prophecy and can fathom all mysteries and all knowledge, and if I have a faith that can move mountains, but do not have love, I am nothing. Love is patient, love is kind . . . Love never fails. But where there are prophecies, they will cease; where there are tongues, they will be stilled; where there is knowledge, it will pass away. For we know in part and we prophesy in part, but when completeness comes, what is in part disappears. . . . For now we see only a reflection as in a mirror; then we shall see face to face. Now I know in part; then I shall know fully, even as I am fully known. And now these three remain: faith, hope and love. But the greatest of these is love.

He set the book down and looked around at the few of us gathered there. Then he said quietly, "Think about a love that is so powerful, so immensely powerful that it does not even need to exert effort to create a universe, because He *is power*. Now think about that kind of power, the greatness of the power that put the stars in the sky and spoke light into being before the sun even was, and now think about that power focused into love for one human person. You. God valued you so immeasurably much that He sent a king to die for you. The King died for you. And He adores you."

The room was still. Our eyes were fixed on Parker, who

seemed to be radiating both vulnerability and ease, as though these words were at once the most intimate and the most self-evident he'd ever spoken. Imagine the way God loves you, he told us. You are completely and totally known. He sees the depths of your heart and your silliest foibles and your most monstrous thoughts and your most generous acts, and He takes it all and He delights in you and loves you, totally and finally.

Right then something happened that I wasn't expecting, which is that I remembered what it feels like to be a Christian, or what it felt like for me. There's a membrane between imagining God's love as a thought experiment and experiencing it as absolute reality, and if you slip across it, the entire known universe shatters and reassembles itself to be more whole and beautiful than you thought was possible. I had forgotten.

It's a tragedy you can't truly explain what this feels like, the safety and wonder and rest and joy and shattering humility and crazy peace, because when you feel it, all you want is for everyone else to feel it, too. It's as though you've been let in on the most magnificent secret and all you want is to bring everyone else along, because if everyone knew the secret it could solve every problem in the world. This is what Christians call, in a terrific understatement, "the Good News." This is also called grace. Sitting in that converted bar, I got maybe seven seconds of a vivid memory of grace, and the memory alone was enough to remind me why people who know the Good News do wild things to spread it: they're filled up with a love so great it demands to be given away.

When the world clicked back into its familiar alignment,

the bar actually looked different. The light was coming in softer, and the room glowed hopeful and clean. Parker was talking about miracles.

As soon as the sermon ended, Jessi and the other girls dumped the untouched waters in garbage bins and pecked at their iPhones. Everyone decided on burritos for lunch. The bar resolved, slowly, back into a bar. Before long, they climbed back into their enormous truck and headed toward the coast.

THE BIG EMPTY

Lately I've been catching myself looking at spaces the way I did when I was a little girl. Up until this strange renaissance, I would not have said that the way I look at rooms or buildings or even a nicely constructed breezeway has changed much since I first started paying attention to my surroundings. But the return of the old way of seeing alerted me to the fact that there once had been an old way and that I had, at some unknown time, lost it.

When I was a child, I inhabited spaces with a basic indifference to the principles of physics, the proportions of my own body, or the fact that the mind cannot actually manifest the contents of its own imagination. I looked at tall buildings as if I could fly.

Take the airplane, for instance: a space that is completely unremarkable because a commercial airplane resembles exactly every other commercial airplane in the world. It doesn't even require description—everyone accustomed to air travel relies on the sensible predictability of airplane interiors, so noticing their particulars (which become, through repeated viewing, not so particular) is unnecessary. I interacted with the inside of the last airplane I took as if there were nothing to look at. I scooted my backpack under the seat in front of me, plugged in my headphones, and turned my attention to what seemed to be the only entertainment at hand: a magazine.

At age seven, I might have looked around and imagined how interesting it would be if someone opened a bodega in the overhead compartment because swinging the door open and shut on that upper hinge (like the door on a DeLorean!) would make for a thrilling beginning and ending to the business day, and people could buy their snacks from you on the way to their seats, and you'd have a great view of everything. Or I might decide that I'd like to scamper underneath the seats, mouselike, navigating people's ankles and luggage as though they were a great, shifting obstacle course. Or I'd spend a while looking at the rounded cups of the rotatable lights above every seat and wonder what it would be like to press your ear to them and hear whispers.

I don't remember when I stopped seeing spaces that way—it had certainly been years since I'd walked into a cathedral and thought idly about what it might feel like to float around up in the dome—but the lapse doesn't seem surprising. I'm less bored as an adult than I was as a child. Or perhaps it would be more accurate to say that I spend less time with nothing to do but look around. I spend less time lying on the floor or hanging upside down from the furniture. I am less frequently granted the opportunity, for want of anything better to do, to pay absolute attention to my surroundings. The twentieth-century philosopher and mystic Simone Weil wrote, "Absolute, unmitigated attention is prayer," and by this logic I have, in becoming an adult, forgotten the art of praying in and over spaces, of praying by looking. No surprise, then, that though I may be less bored, a world without airplane bodegas seems more boring.

Lots of people lose the knack for attention and imagination that came easily to them as children. Adults have more practice occupying the world than children, and our engagement is necessarily more practical and programmatic. Inasmuch as we retain the skill of absolute visual attention, we confine its practice to certain spaces, set apart for that exact purpose. Museums, like churches, are places dedicated for this kind of awareness, places where we enter an impressive quietude and only look. Even then, the exhibit at hand tends to be something within the space—a painting, a relic—rather than the space itself.

For much of 2012, the most popular art exhibit in New York was a mostly empty fifty-five-thousand-square-foot hall roughly the size and style of a nineteenth-century European train station. This is the Park Avenue Armory, a contemporary art exhibition space that used to be, a century and a half ago, the drill hall for the Seventh Regiment of the National Guard. It's the size of Grand Central, but without anything in it. This amount of empty space in Manhattan is spectacular, and the mutability of the Armory, the way it's available for adaptation by whatever artist or jewelry brand or opera collective installs work within it, elevates it almost to the realm of the mystical. Whatever goes in there, people notice.

The piece that caused a stir in 2012 was *the event of a thread* by Ann Hamilton, an artist known for enormous, hypersensory multimedia installations. Before arriving at the Armory, Hamilton had filled an impressively large old warehouse space at MASS MoCA with seven million slips of paper, which fluttered down from the rafters one at a time at roughly the pace of human breathing, one slip per breath, until the floors were so covered that visitors had to wade. She had overseen the construction of a 118-foot-long meditation boat, modeled after the abandoned walking meditation halls of Luang Prabang monasteries. She had made a metalworker's house in Japan "sing" by fitting it with accordions attached to pulleys that sighed with the wind, and rigging the stone kiln with rubber hoses so visitors could "play" the kiln by blowing them. She had installed Leslie speakers in a restored nineteenth-century barn in Knislinge, Sweden, so that a voice—singing, humming, calling, and reading aloud—created a pathway through the otherwise empty building. Hamilton's art practice is, among other things, nurturing an imaginative relationship with space.

When interviewed, Hamilton often uses language indicating that she thinks of spaces as living things. She usually works on commission now, which means that she makes installations knowing the exact warehouse or gallery it's destined for, and she talks, without irony, about the fact that she begins working by "listening" to these places and taking her cues from them. She looks for evidence of the bodies that have passed through already—worn places in the floor, burnished door handles. MASS MoCA in its hugeness and silence (once a factory for dyeing textiles) invited an exploration of the connection between voice and void, empty space and the potential of creating words or sounds to fill it. All the slips of paper falling down at the pace of breath, she says, were either empty-of-words or full-of-space, much like breath itself. As it accumulated over days the paper blanketed the warehouse in an overwhelm of both presence and void. Hamilton called the project *corpus*, and unofficially, "the big empty." "It's not something to consume," she told a *New York Times* reporter in 2004, "but something you have to wait for. So it's actually very full, filled by you and the collected memories of your body in time and space."

These kinds of dualities appeal to Hamilton: the edge between somethingness and nothingness; the way empty space can be a humming, breathing potentiality or a gaping absence. Usually she involves the human body to explore these contradictions, as with *stylus*, an installation that included enormous video close-ups of moving hands, or *aloud*, which featured vaguely grotesque close-up photographs of the mouths of figures on medieval wood altarpieces. She has also turned the body itself into her exhibition space: she imagines her mouth as a room and uses a small pinhole camera held between her teeth to take a picture of it. She attaches a miniature surveillance camera to her hand and runs it over a photograph or object to see what happens when one sense and organ (touch, hand) is transformed into another (sight, eye).

At the Park Avenue Armory, Hamilton's installation focused on crossings between near and far: a writer's hand crossing paper, a voice crossing a room, bodies crossing space. The drill hall was turned into a field of swings, hung seventy feet from arched iron trusses and attached to a vast white silk cloth, twice the width of the space and folded back on itself. The swings held the cloth aloft, and people were invited to swing on them, which activated a rope-and-pulley system and stirred the silk to wide, gentle undulations. There were forty-two radios in paper bags for visitors to carry around, broadcasting short lines of text. A flock of homing pigeons surrounded readers, seated at a refectory table stationed at one end of the hall, unrolling scrolls of Aristotle and Darwin. At the other end of the hall, a young woman wrote letters to lightness.

In this space, people seemed reduced—or maybe magnified—to childlike engagement. They swung high on the swings and laughed in delight, craning their necks to see the way the wires and pulleys crisscrossed in the air far overhead. They lay on their backs underneath the curtain for hours, unprompted, watching how the cloth swayed in the light. They ran through the hall with paper bags full of sound, and paused occasionally to lift them to their ears and hear whispers. They looked and they looked. They paid absolute attention.

A few years after *the event of a thread* left the Armory, I took the train to Philadelphia to see Hamilton's newest project, *habitus, a commonplace*, on the Delaware River waterfront. Like *the event of a thread*, it was a large-scale meditation on material—this time, upon the relationship between cloth and language. "Habitus" is a sociological term for the way habits of body and mind are created by imitating those around you, and the way groups of people form coherent social practices, and Hamilton wanted to experiment with cloth and words as a metaphor for the way we are bound and held from birth in materials made by the hands of other people.

The installation took place, once again, in a warehouse, only this time the space was exposed to the elements and situated near a river. Giant swirling curtains of Tyvek, arranged on hoops and spinning like dervishes, hung throughout the space, waiting for people to step inside and be enveloped. Visitors could make them spin by pulling a series of woven wool sallies, but often the wind would rise and take control of the installation.

Habitus, Hamilton writes, "is the landscape made from letting go and holding on, from reelings and turnings, unravelings and gatherings, spinning and scrolling, continuous and discontinuous threads, in circles and in lines." In practice, the exhibit looked a lot like play: people stood in the center of the columns of fabric, looking up and laughing. Others yanked up and down on sallies like old-fashioned bell ringers. One reviewer noted, "Adults aren't usually offered such fun."

In the initial critical reception of *the event of a thread* and *habitus*, there was skepticism about whether all the audience participation bespoke artistic seriousness. Roberta Smith in *The New York Times* suggested, a little snidely, that *the event of a thread* might not be art at all but participatory theater, a sociological experiment, or the beginning of a new fitness craze: aerobic swinging classes. But visitors to Hamilton's installations tend to spend much longer looking at her work than people look at artwork on average. At *the event of a thread* people stayed for hours.

Lately, I feel as if I can't get enough space. I don't know if I can blame this problem on New York, but it is a perfect problem to blame on New York, with its sharp-nosed skyscrapers, the obliteration of horizon lines, the violation of personal dignity perpetrated by the 4 train at rush hour. "We worried, some of us, about what might happen to our brains," wrote the writer Amy Benson of moving to New York. "How could we think when we knew that in every direction, for miles, millions of people were also thinking?"

Saying I can't get enough space is just another way of saying that I'm not thinking very well and that this problem of thinking feels at least partially spatial. If you conceive of the mind as a thing that has dimensionality, something that when you close your eyes seems to stretch up and out and behind and beyond you, then it is easy to imagine the mind as a place that one can move about in, and that this movement can be directional or aimless, wandering or purposeful. One can imagine that space as bounded but vaguely so, defined by parameters that are either shifting or unknown. There are days when this space of the mind feels expansive and clean, like the horizon line at the Pacific. And there are days—or weeks, or months—when its landscape is reduced to the size of an antique shop, suffocated by teetering stacks of chairs and dusty old keys amassed in plastic buckets under scratched records going for a dollar each.

The pleasure and—if we can call it this—radicalism of Hamilton's work is that she makes you feel somehow the largeness of the space and the story in your mind, and the smallness of your body and your story in the world—and that you are alive and space is alive and the two of you, you and space, are doing this thing together. If you're doing it together, you can push and pull the space inside you by engaging differently, more imaginatively, with the space outside you.

Which suggests, possibly, that if you are stuck somewhere small in your mind, somewhere unhappy or afraid or paralyzed or heartbroken, all of which are a kind of claustrophobic circling and circling, you might be able to reverse-engineer an expansion, shove yourself through into some larger mind place by putting yourself in the way of some vaster spaces in the world. At least I think that's so.

GOOD KARMA

Keeler, California, is so far away that when you scan the radio for a station, it dials through empty airwaves until it comes all the way around to your original blank frequency, and goes again. I was driving south to north through the center of the state on the hunt for someplace remote and dry, extreme, unlike any of the landscapes familiar to me. I was following the grand American tradition of running westward from my problems. A photographer friend had told me to see Owens Lake in Keeler, and from what the map was telling me, it also looked like Keeler was the last place to get gas for a while. The roads had gotten progressively empty as I'd driven from Los Angeles, up through the canyons of wind turbines beating steadily against the morning. The land desiccated and lop-sided shanties began to appear by the side of the highway, their windows blown out and graffiti tracing their walls. By the time I got to Keeler I hadn't seen another town in a long time.

There was no gas station there, and no place for coffee. Instead, I found rows of abandoned homes and trailers. Stripped cars, broken refrigerators, pieces of a printer, wood shacks, tin shacks, brick shacks—even, I think, some plastic shacks. The buildings were situated in rows, sort of, which lent the effect of streets, but nothing was paved. Despite all the cars and all the stuff, there were no people. Nothing was moving. The sign said POPULATION: 50.

I went through the streets slowly, past an abandoned tractor, empty gas cartons, rusted kitchen appliances, a school bus retrofitted for living in, furnished with dusty rugs and an upright piano. Cats.

Out past the piles of wood was eighty miles of lake bed: sand and dunes, little tufts of desert grass and dead weeds. To the west lay the Sierra Nevada mountain range; to the east, Death Valley.

A hundred years ago, my friend had told me, Keeler was lakefront property, and the valley where it sits was so idyllic, so lush and rugged with ocotillo and sage and snowcapped peaks in the distance, that Hollywood used the land to shoot all its most famous Westerns. If Owens Lake and the valley it sits in look vaguely familiar, it's because when you close your eyes and imagine the mythic American West, you're imagining this place in a past life. Hopalong Cassidy rode here, and the Lone Ranger, and The Duke with his creaky swagger.

It is still stunning land, air clear as a bell, mountains on the horizon, uninterrupted gradient of sunlight, but the lake is gone. In 1913, worried about its own water supply, the city of Los Angeles diverted Owens Lake through its aqueduct; by 1926, the valley was dry. People abandoned the area so quickly that nobody bothered to take down the road sign that warns people entering Keeler of flooding. Hollywood still uses this area as a backdrop, but it no longer passes for America. Instead, it's used for movies set in Afghanistan, on alien planets, or in postapocalyptic wastelands. The local film commissioner, who's less busy now than he used to be, reported that someone had recently shot a porn movie in town titled *The Hills Have Thighs*.

Eventually, I found someone, a man standing beside a sign reading DICKHEAD PARKING ONLY, pulling things out of his truck. His name was Luke—he was a seasonal hire out from Montana working on what he referred to as dust "ameniga-tion." "You're standing in the worst dust bowl in the country," he hooted, leaning into my car through the passenger-side window. "The wind comes through the valley so fast that it kicks up arsenic dust storms so bad you can't see." Owens Lake blows four million tons of dust every year, and the chemicals that occur naturally in the lake bed (arsenic, cadmium, and nickel) make poison wind. The street that leads out into the lake bed, past an outpost of the Los Angeles Department of Power and Water, is called Sulfate Road.

Fifteen years ago, California earmarked four hundred million dollars to do something about it, a number that has since grown to two billion dollars. First they tried to reirrigate, Luke told me, to see if water could tamp down the dust. But they couldn't keep the soil wet. "They still do that some," he said, "but there'll never be water here again." His job, he said, was to carry tarps out into the lake bed every day and fasten them to the ground.

"What are you doing here?" he asked, eyeing me. When I told him I was looking for gas, he laughed and waved his hand northward. "You gotta go to Lone Pine," he said, leaning back out of my window. "Take care, kiddo." Then, as I was driving away, he waved at me. "Don't drink the water," he yelled. "It's contaminated."

I stopped the car. "Didn't I just pass the Crystal Geyser plant on my way up here?"

"Yeah," he said. "Drink that instead."

The American interstates are a wonderful place to be outside of yourself, and a convenient place to be unmoored. "Driving is a spectacular form of amnesia," wrote Jean Baudrillard of driving through America. "Everything is to be discovered, everything to be obliterated." Driving through the American West produces "a kind of invisibility, transparency, or transversality in things, simply by emptying them out." There is the sense that you're driving through a gigantic metaphor—the landscape is so preposterously large, you've seen it so many times in books and movies about grand and perilous American journeys. You've seen the figure in this story before, making her way across the desert, driven by motivations that echo. The figure is now you, you are now her, moving through not so much a real place as a corner of the collective unconscious. It's all pleasantly and unnervingly surreal, or hyperreal, like living a story that's already been written.

The Lone Pine visitor center was selling copies of *Wild* in the gift shop. The Pacific Crest Trail passes roughly twenty miles west of town, and Cheryl Strayed's memoir of escaping death and finding herself via a thousand-mile hike through this terrain had just been released as a blockbuster movie (shot in Oregon, not locally). The visitor center seemed designed both to romanticize the prospect and to warn against romanticizing too optimistically. Their exhibits offered panel after panel of illustrated warnings about how dangerous this landscape can be and stressing the idiocy of going anywhere unprepared. Hike the walking trails that have reopened along the lake bed and enjoy the birds that have begun to reappear there, the signage suggested, but be vigilant. There's wind that will come over you and blot the world out with dust, the literature explained, and there's no water. There are predatory animals. When I walked back outside, there was a crow pecking around my car.

As Luke promised, Lone Pine had paved roads, a store where you can buy food, and motels. It also had four restaurants, a "bookstore" that mostly sells kitsch and mineral samples, a graveyard, a bar, two gas stations, a high school, and a film museum honoring the history of Hollywood. I checked into the Dow Villa Motel, which looked comfortable if vaguely eerie. The room was lined with photographs of cowboys on film sets. The proprietor of the hotel was excited to tell me that his grandmother was John Wayne's "town girlfriend" when he came in for shoots.

The people who continue to live in Lone Pine do so even though it's a place without a future. As Luke said, there will never be water here again because the state of California has decided that this land should be dry so that the cities on the coast can forget that they occupy desert as well—so that there can be orange trees in the irrigated backyards of Los Angeles.

It seems unlikely that there will ever be much industry or infrastructure in this part of the state again. The land can't grow anything and so it's not worth anything, except to the people who have always lived on it and always will. They stay out of stubbornness, or stuckness, or perhaps out of a refusal to believe that the water won't return even though everyone knows it's impossible. Someday, and maybe soon, water will stop coming out of the tap in Lone Pine, as it has elsewhere in California during the worst of the droughts—Los Angeles still diverts water from the Central Valley to suit its needs, so parts of the state go all the way dry.

Until then, there are three things to do: they work occasionally for the movie crews that come out, when they come out; they walk out into the lake bed every day and lay down rocks and tarp to keep the dust down; or they work at the Crystal Geyser plant, bottling water for the rest of America. (The plant's water comes from nearby Olancha, which receives runoff from the Sierra Nevada; until 2014, Crystal Geyser Olancha kept its wastewater runoff in a pond they called Arsenic Pond until the California Department of Toxic Substances Control determined it was hazardous waste.)

There's a peculiar social energy that crops up among people who live in annihilating landscapes. There's a looseness of speech that comes from assuming no one outside the community is listening, or assuming that since most of reality is happening elsewhere, this slice of it can go about its business unnoticed. In the coffee shop, I met a woman wearing flip-flops whom people were calling the mayor, though I couldn't tell if she was actually the mayor or if that was just because she knew everybody. When she welcomed me to Lone Pine, she kissed me on the forehead and blessed me. "You come back now," she said, moving on to another table.

In the evening, I went to the local dive bar to play pool—a trick for making conversation—and met an old man who wanted to tell me about his glorious karma. "I don't lie, cheat, or steal," he said proudly. "I don't drink, smoke, or do any kind of drug. I did all that until seven years ago, and then I decided to turn it around. This is my last life on earth, and I'm doing this one right."

His name was Jeremiah. I asked him if he could read other people's karma, too, and he said he couldn't, but he could give good karma. "Can you give bad karma?" I asked. He said yes he could, and I smiled. "Better not make you angry."

"No, no," he said, smiling. "I love you. You're going to have a beautiful life."

"How do you know?" I asked.

"I can just tell," he said. "Your life is going to be beautiful." I thought about that for a minute, and then he asked, "Isn't it?"

"Hm?"

"Isn't it already?"

I groped for a response.

Then he told me the reason he could bestow karma was that he had been abducted by aliens when he was seven.

I went back outside and looked at the one stoplight.

I got in my car and drove out into the mountains, which did look like the West and the moon at the same time, and perhaps like Afghanistan. The rock formations were voluptuous, like the bodies of sleeping women. As the sun was dipping, I drove south past Lone Pine, past Keeler, and took a right on Sulfate Road.

When I stepped out of the car, the dirt beneath my feet crumbled and lifted gently into the air. I walked the rest of the way out into the middle of the lake bed, a white plain dotted with tufts of grass and bedded in places with gravel. I paused. Twilight came.

Eventually I sat in the dust, cross-legged, and took out an orange from my backpack. As I peeled it, drops of juice fell to the dirt and vanished, and a sticker came off on my hand. I turned it over to pull it off: PRODUCT OF CALIFORNIA.

HABITUS

The dresses take a year to sew, and the girls spend a year learning how to wear them; how to glide, how to hold their arms out so they never touch the skirts, how to hold their heads under the weight of the period-appropriate coiffure. The look is Marie Antoinette in her let-them-eat-cake days, and the dresses, like Marie's dresses, weigh so much—up to one hundred pounds—that they hurt the girl wearing them. They leave bruises at the shoulders and hips where the dress bones pull down on girl bones. The longest and hardest task is learning to sink to the floor gracefully and rise again as if the monument on their hips were only a trick of light. The dresses, like the gestures, are passed down from mother to daughter.

Each girl needs five dressers, who lace her into her corset first, then affix the "cage" of the hoop skirt to her waist, sneaking a pillow between the cage and her body so her skin isn't rubbed raw. Then come the petticoats, and the dress on top of that. She is dressed over a tarp, and once everything is in place, the women pick up the girl and the tarp all together and walk her to the stage so that the dress never touches the ground. If it is raining outside, they wrap her in plastic, too.

When she walks, she takes the smallest steps possible so that she appears to be borne along on a current of air. Large steps make the giant hooped skirt slap back and forth, which is not desirable, and anyway a stately, exhibitive gait is key. She holds her arms always at attention, hovering lightly above the hips of the dress, elbows soft, wrists tilted, hands in the Barbie claw. This is a staple of the contemporary pageant, the ritual gestures, all bodies made to form the same shapes—back rod-straight in the corset, head erect, smile broad.

The crowning touch is the curtsy, for which the girls practice at length, and which they taught me in a group in the salon, all of them laughing in flip-flops and sweatpants with their toenails and lip liner already done. They showed me how you go slowly to one knee and then, while remaining motionless from the waist up, tuck the other knee underneath for extra support. Slowly, we sat down and back on our heels and bowed magisterially over our imaginary skirts, keeping our chins up up up until the last moment, when you finally accede to the skirt, turning the right cheek. In the dresses, it looks in this final phase like the girl is pressing a gentle ear to her dress, listening for what's underneath.

Why? I asked. Why is this the bow?

They shrugged. It's always been. That's how they taught it to us.

There are many debutante balls in Texas, and even a number of pageants that use historical costumes, but the Society of Martha Washington Colonial Pageant and Ball in Laredo, Texas, is the most opulently patriotic among them. In the mid-1800s, a number of European American settlers from the East were sent to staff a new military base in Laredo, Texas, a region that had only recently, and violently, been annexed by the United States. They found themselves in a place that was tenuously and unenthusiastically American. Feeling perhaps a little forlorn at being so starkly in the minority, these new arrivals established a local chapter of the lamentably named Improved Order of Red Men. (They dressed as "Indians," called their officers "chiefs," and began their meetings, or "powwows," by banging a tomahawk instead of a gavel.)

A distant offshoot of the Sons of Liberty, the Improved Order of Red Men fashioned itself as a torchbearer for colonial-era American patriotism, and its young Laredo chapter was particularly eager to enshrine that culture down at the border. So the Washington's Birthday Celebration Association (WBCA) was formed. For the inaugural celebration in 1898, they "laid siege" to the Old Laredo City Hall, pretending to be a warring native tribe conquering the city. (The optics here must have been confusing, as the Order was comprised of white men while most of the city's residents were either Mexican by birth

or indigenous.) A young woman was appointed to play Pocahontas, and after brokering peace between the tribe and the
city, she received the keys to Laredo in appreciation for her
efforts.

The siege was done away with long ago, but every February
since 1898, the Washington's Birthday Celebration Association
has thrown a massive festival—America's most elaborate
homage to its first president. There's a Comedy Jam for
George, a Founding Father's 5k Fun Run, a jalapeño festival,
a Princess Pocahontas Pageant, an Anheuser-Busch-sponsored
citywide parade, and so on. The prestige event of the season is
the pageant and debutante ball hosted by the Society of Martha
Washington, which was started by WBCA wives in 1940 with
the aim of adding glitz to the festival. Their daughters dress up
in what is imagined to be Martha-like attire, playacting historical figures who might have known her. Each year, one society
member is honored with the opportunity to play Martha herself, and a man from the WBCA plays George.

The WBCA was started by a white upper class, but in the
hundred years since its founding, the population of Laredo has
become almost entirely mixed-ethnicity, with 96 percent of the
population identified on the census as "Hispanic." Through inter-
marriage, the upper class of Laredo has come to include not only
the Lyndeckers and the Bunns (two original WBCA families
still prominent in the Society) but also families named Rodri-
guez, Gutierrez, Martinez, and Reyes. Today, Martha, George,
and the girls are mostly Mexican American. Many of them descend from the original WBCA families, but just as many descend
from the people who were categorically oppressed—and at times

massacred—by an American colonialist expansion set in motion by the founding fathers they dress up to honor.

Two months after hearing a rumor about a borderlands debutante ball where Mexican American girls dress up in full period costume and pretend to be Martha Washington, I arrived in Laredo from the north. I'd flown into San Antonio, where my grandmother lives, and driven the 150 miles of interstate down to the border. When I checked into my hotel, the front desk attendant warned me not to miss the last exit on the freeway. If you don't get off at the last exit, she said, there's no turning around and you'll wind up across in Nuevo Laredo and need a passport to get back. "It's okay," I assured her. "I'm from a border city, too."

Laredo and Nuevo Laredo are often described as neighboring cities, but geographically they are one city, the Laredo–Nuevo Laredo Metropolitan Area, bisected by the border and the river, a city that's American on its north side and Mexican on the south. The Rio Grande is narrow as a straight pin at this portion of its journey from Colorado to the Gulf of Mexico; only fifty yards across. It's a city of bridges: there are four international bridges across the river and more under construction. Thousands of people cross from one place to the next each day, to work or go to school or see family that lives on the other side. Laredo's adopted nickname is "the Gateway City," though the border is tightly regulated.

Of the major ports of trade, trafficking, and immigration between the United States and Mexico, Laredo is among the very busiest, often outranked only by San Diego, California, where I am from.

There are some common features of major border towns in this country. They contain armies of immigration enforcement officers; if you drive down near the border, you'll see ICE vehicles ferrying migrants between detention centers. Everyone knows people who are undocumented, which lately means that everyone knows someone who has vanished without warning or notice. The radio traffic reports always include estimates for the delays at each of the crossings. There's the fence.

Unlike Laredo, San Diego remains majority white and quite segregated in ways that were designed by city planners and codified by city councils decades ago. Speaking generally, white and affluent people—categories that overlap almost entirely there—populate the west and north of the county, the parts that have the beaches. While all beaches in California are public land, people who own beachfront property own the views of the ocean. They own the right to see horizon. With some exceptions, lower-income families, immigrants, and most Mexican Americans live south and east, on the sides of the county that face the desert and the border.

I was a teenager when I first went to the beach at Border Field State Park with some friends and we meandered all the way until we ran into the fence. I was startled to see the wooden posts jammed deep in the sand, and to see them extending out into the ocean. This reveals more than I wish it did about the teenager I was and the city I lived in: I'd never known that the border went beyond the water's edge because I'd never seen it.

Every Easter, we would travel as a family to Mission, Texas, which is about an hour southeast of Laredo, farther down into the Valley, as Texans call it. Mission is a border town, too, but it has none of the wealth of the port cities. Hidalgo County, which holds Mission, where my great-grandparents lived, and where my grandparents were raised, and where my mother spent long passages of her childhood, is consistently ranked among the poorest counties in the United States. My earliest memories of Mission are of my great-grandma Carmen's clothesline; billboards with letters missing; a dusty pickup with a bed full of watermelons.

The family would gather each Easter in Mission at my great-grandparents' house. There were always so many people that we'd have to go to a park for the proper picnic. My mother is one of seven, her parents were one of seven and one of six, respectively, and there were so many cousins and second cousins and cousins removed, great-uncles and great-aunts and in-laws, passels of babies—and Grandma Carmen, eighty-something and scraping five feet tall, making tortillas by hand for everyone.

It is a tradition among Mexican families in South Texas to do the Easter egg hunt with *cascarones*, eggshells that have been hollowed out, filled with paper confetti, and resealed with colorful tissue paper. Once the children have hunted all the *cascarones*, there's a smashing melee, where everyone runs around and cracks the eggs over one another's heads so the confetti explodes in showers around you, settling into your hair and sandals. Some people, like my grandmother Maria Elena, refused to ruin their carefully set hair, and were generally known to be off-limits. Others, like Grandma Carmen, turned it into a sport, tackling to the ground any young uncles who'd evaded capture and giving them a confetti head rub. At the end, everyone would be in stitches laughing, and inevitably one child would be bawling, and the ground of that corner of Mission would look as if a parade had blown through. As a child, I spent a lot of time playing in the colorful, littered dirt of that park, and understood it to be, in some important ways, dirt that belonged to me, and me to it.

Still, I always felt slightly out of place in Mission. My father is a somewhat undetermined WASP mix by way of New Jersey, and when I was young I looked mostly like him. There's a picture of me from my first Easter in Mission, standing between two twin girls, the daughters of my mother's best friend from elementary school. At two years old I look so fair and large next to them that a friend once saw the photo and said, laughing, "Who's that big white baby?"

The last time we went to stay with Grandma Carmen, I was a teenager, and spent the whole time feeling pale and giant. I was still getting used to having grown such a different body from my mother's. I looked even less like her aunts and cousins, and as we gathered at Grandma Carmen's table in a warm haze of laughter and rapid Spanish, I wished I could belong there. I was already a half foot taller than these women, pale and freckled, with the type of features that had recently led a friend's mother to refer to me as "that German Jewish girl."

There's a photo of us together standing outside her front

door, Grandma Carmen and my brother and me. He's thirteen and I'm fifteen and next to us she looks like a child, barely four foot eleven, barely ninety pounds. My brother looks plausibly related to her; I look like a guest. We didn't talk much, but she would grasp me by my arms and peer into my eyes and smile. I remember her in her kitchen, holding my mother's hands and laughing, saying, *Mi'ja, no se lo que les gustan comer.* I don't know what your children like to eat. Always, we would get on a plane, and fly back to the ocean.

I met Martha Washington at a strip mall in north Laredo, where we had agreed to have lunch in between her nail appointment and her hair appointment. Every year, the Society of Martha Washington chooses from among its ranks a woman who will play "Martha" for the year, and 2018's Martha, Tami Summers, was two days away from concluding her duties.

"Right now I'm kinda nervous because of all the stuff that's going on," Tami said, waving vaguely at her stomach. She ordered bone broth and a piece of chicken. "I don't want to sound silly, but I try to get things organized because I'm a teacher, and I plan. And then everything goes to hell." The Martha Washington–themed T-shirts she'd ordered hadn't arrived until eleven o'clock the night before, which delayed the arrangement of the welcome baskets she'd planned for the few dozen family members arriving from out of town to see her in the pageant. "So that's running late. And then I had a mani, so my nails are done, and I have to be back at the Civic Center at three, because we're putting on the dresses to see how they work onstage. And then we practice tonight with the dresses on." She heaved a little sigh, and took a sip of coffee.

Tami is gregarious and forceful, a short woman with wide blue eyes, a broad, friendly face, and the demeanor of someone who's made a career of corralling teenagers. Her hair was, for the moment, bright blond, which isn't how she normally wears it. The stylist who does hair for the pageant wanted her to go platinum for Martha. (Martha's hair was brown, but that's not the point.) "I kind of like it," Tami said, patting her head. "I think I might keep it this way."

She wore a crisp white button-down embroidered with the blue crest of the Society. Across from her sat her childhood friend Carole, also a member of the Society, and to her right sat her teenage daughter, Bailey, who apologized right away for how much she would be yawning through lunch. She'd flown in from Florence, where she'd just started a semester abroad.

"I had to bring her home," Tami said, laughing.

"I was there not even two weeks. Maybe ten days," Bailey said, rolling her eyes. "I thought about missing it, but it's one of those things."

"It's like a wedding," Tami added. "It's really kind of crazy and over the top."

Most women are members of the Society because someone in their family was in it—a mother, an aunt—or because they marry into it. Tami's husband's aunt was a founding member, his father played George in 1987, and he played George in 2006. Tami, who is naturally enthusiastic, a joiner, was admitted into the group in 1998. Plenty of Society daughters decide they don't want to debut and let the tradition end with their mothers, despite any pressure from family to continue the legacy, but Bailey required no convincing. She began practicing the elaborate curtsy of the Martha Washington debutantes when she was three years old.

There can be only a set number of members in the Society at any given time (about 250), and openings for new members are always outpaced by the number of women who wish to join, which is why women are encouraged to apply for membership long before their daughters are of debutante age. New members are admitted only when existing members either die or retire, so one expects to spend several years on the waiting list. Once admitted off the waitlist, each new member must sell fifteen thousand dollars of advertisements in the pageant's annual program, for two years in a row. The program is the size, shape, style, and layout of a giant high school yearbook.

I asked the three women how they understood the Society's role in the community more generally. Tami paused, chewing and thinking. "It's interesting here in Laredo because we're such a Hispanic population. At least 95 percent. It's really a Hispanic base, which is how the WBCA started. We were so Hispanic and so Mexican and so far away, located on the border—we were saying to America, 'We are American, and we're going to celebrate Washington's birthday!' We are dual culture. We embrace our Mexican roots."

This wasn't my understanding of the origins of the Association—that it was started by Mexicans hoping to be brought into the feel-goodery of the American body politic— but as I was considering my next question Carole chimed in, pointing out that, in her view, the crowning event of the Washington's Birthday Celebration is something called the Abrazo ceremony, which takes place the morning after the pageant. Four children, two from Laredo and two from Nuevo Laredo, cross the Juarez-Lincoln International Bridge from their respective sides, dressed in colonial-era costumes and accompanied by the mayors of their cities. When they reach each other in the middle of the bridge, over the waters of the Rio Grande, they hug.

"This whole celebration is about unification and friendship, especially with our neighbors to the south," said Carole. "I think for you, knowing you," she said, nodding at Tami, "the number one thing about this celebration is connection and family. I mean, for god's sake, Bailey is here from Italy."

Tami agreed. "I just think the connection and the continuation of the thing—"

Carole interrupted. "It's roots. Not connection."

"But what does a root do?" Tami asked. "It connects you to the ground. It connects you to the earth. It connects you to other people."

Bailey nodded, looking at her mom. "It makes you a part of something."

I spent most of the next two days in salons, particularly in Regis Salon at the Mall del Norte, where Tami and a number of the debutantes were having their hair prepared for the various events of the weekend: the dress rehearsal, the pageant, the parade, the cocktail reception. When I arrived, the salon's rather stern-looking owner, a woman named Grace, was in the middle of back-combing Tami's hair sky high. Blond extensions lay like coiled rope on a metal tray nearby.

Tami grinned in greeting, careful not to move her head. Her iPhone was in her lap, and she was steadily fielding questions and minor crises from the various people needing her attention. Next to Tami, a dark-haired, skinny sixteen-year-old named Sydney was further along—the young stylist working on her was already pinning her extensions in a pompadour. Sydney's mother was negotiating with a makeup artist about the day's schedule. I asked her what it was like to have a daughter presented.

She smiled. "It's been a beautiful experience. She's loving it, she gets pampered, she shines at the parties." The three of them began to walk me through the slate of social obligations that precede the pageant: There's a formal father-daughter gala in November, where the girls wear white ball gowns like traditional debutantes. Then, throughout the year, each of the fifteen girls is allowed to throw up to three private parties for the other debutantes and their parents. It's customary for them to be elaborate, with themes like "Breakfast at Tiffany's." For Sydney's Chanel-themed party, they said, all the girls had received little Chanel bags as party favors.

Sydney's mom leaned forward to show me a picture of Sydney in her dress for the November father-daughter dance. It was a long white satin gown, off the shoulder. "It's actually a wedding gown," she said.

"It looks like one," I offered.

"Yes. You have to buy a wedding dress. And because I

have an older daughter, too, I now basically own two wedding dresses." She laughed.

I sat for a while, watching Grace clip extensions into Tami's hair and mentally calculating. "Tami, since you're the Martha, does the Society pay for these appointments?"

Tami shook her head and pointed at her chest.

"You pay for it."

"Yes. The Society pays for . . . nothing."

"Not the dresses."

"No, no. That's why you'll see all levels of dresses. You'll see ones where you can tell they spent a lot of money on it and some where . . . they can get really crazy and be really reasonable just depending on what the person's budget is. We have to sponsor our float in the parade. We pay for our tickets, we pay for our dress. There are yearly dues."

"Are there scholarships for members who want their daughters to be presented but don't have the money to do it?"

"No, no, no. No. No, they just either don't do it or they borrow a dress. And some people will say, 'We just can't do it.' If it comes down to either you're gonna get a car or you're going to college or you're going to get presented, you don't do it."

"Do you have to have a different outfit for every party?"

Tami laughed. "Oh, yeah! And shoes."

Bailey chimed in. "And hair and makeup."

"And we bought ninety-five seats for friends and family."

I did more math: that morning, I'd paid Tami two hundred dollars for a spare set of tickets to the pageant, ball, and cocktail party. Seeing the look on my face, she snorted in agreement.

"Head up," commanded Grace.

I turned to Sydney. "What's your favorite part of this?"

"Well, I really love the dress," she said. "I'm really in love with it."

"And what's the hardest part?"

She gave a little sigh, and said that the hardest part was wearing the dress. "The weight is on my hips and it's more than sixty pounds," she said. "It really hurts."

That night, back in my hotel room, I started researching the Laredo economy. While the city is one of the least "white" cities in America, a University of Toronto study also names Laredo as the most economically segregated small city in America. In 2014, Laredo processed twenty billion dollars in trade with Mexico, but nearly 40 percent of the city's population lives below the poverty line. The wealthy live in neighborhoods like Plantation, Regency, and Lakeside. The poor live in neighborhoods like El Rincon de Diablo and El Trompe. The per capita income in Laredo is $16,642, and the median household income is $41,302—which is, if your tastes are expensive, roughly the cost of a dress for a Martha.

For the month of February, Texas A&M International University in Laredo loaned gallery space to the Society of Martha Washington to make a museum of retired dresses. Between salon appointments, I drove over to have a look and was greeted by a fishbowl-like room situated on the second floor of the fine arts center. Several dozen mannequins stood silently in full regalia.

Standing in the museum of the dresses gave me the distant feeling of standing among the discarded, gleaming exoskeletons of specific eighteen-year-olds as they existed throughout the twentieth century. You can see how short- or long-waisted the woman was, and the set of her hips, the approximate fleshiness of her upper arms. One dress, with mint-green satin and aurora crystals, holds the shadow-body of Molly LaMantia, who was eighteen in 2011, and her four older sisters before her. Another holds the echo of Evelyn Bruni Summers, a distant in-law of Tami's, who in 1988 had thin wrists and sloping shoulders. My favorite, an especially beautiful gown made of plum brocade with cap sleeves, held a girl whose name I couldn't find but who was uncommonly long-legged and slender.

They are flabbergastingly intricate up close, more beautiful than they need to be. Just as it is a point of pride to have a dress that has been worn by many generations, mostly because it indicates a longer Society lineage, it's also customary to dramatically redesign an inherited dress for every new girl so that it feels uniquely hers. This is also a way of making sure a dress keeps up, as the gowns trend more splendid each year. One series of photographs showed a single gown transform as it was handed down through a set of five sisters. The oldest sister, Reina Ann LaMantia Cullen, had a pearlescent gown with large pink roses embroidered on the bodice and skirt; the next year, her sister Morgan changed the body of the dress to a sea-foam green and added a wide, tongue-pink ribbon; the third sister added a giant bow and replaced the sleeves; the fourth sister threw out all the pink and added olive-green velvet trim; the final sister tore off all the ribbon, added puff sleeves, and let the beadwork, which had been growing steadily more elaborate, shine for itself.

Back in my hotel room, I turned on the television and was greeted by *Say Yes to the Dress*, which appears to have been granted by the state of Texas its own 24/7 channel. *Say Yes to the Dress* is a reality show based at a bridal boutique in Manhattan, and it follows brides who are in search of what is often called "the dream dress." In this search, they are stewarded primarily by Randy Fenoli, a man with an immaculately gelled crew cut. Randy credits his success as both a bridal-wear designer and bride handler to his former life as what was then called a "female impersonator" by the name of Brandi Alexander, who was crowned in the Miss Gay America pageant of 1990. Drag pageantry, Randy once told a journalist, is how he learned to speak to women preparing to be on display.

"These lines are amazing for your curves!" yells Randy to a woman who compares herself to the Chrysler Building.

"I deal with meddling moms in my sleep," he reassures a girl whose mother is dead set against pink.

The camera zooms in and out of fitting rooms, stockrooms, and the grand showroom, where women stand on pedestals in front of small committees of girlfriends or sisters or gay male friends or occasionally a father and almost always a mother. There is invariably one member of the committee deputized to have narrowed eyes and an unpleasant demeanor, and to say things like "I don't think it's doing great things for your ass," or "I think tuck ruffles are whorish."

The presiding philosophy of *Say Yes to the Dress* is that a wedding marks the most important day of a woman's life, not because she's going to marry the person of her dreams but because she is going to wear the dress of her dreams. The wedding day is the day of the perfect dress and, by extension, the apex of a woman's individual beauty, which is one way of measuring the apex of her existence.

I love this show.

I wish I didn't love this show, because I'm allergic to the ideas about women—and gay men, and marriage—it's built on. Women as creatures in pursuit of a princess fantasy or a supermodel fantasy; gay men as effete handmaidens to and quiet manipulators of straight women's vanity; weddings as a performance of heteronormative habit and class aspiration and unbridled consumption. What a nightmare. Still, I can't get enough of it, and part of the reason I love it is because I like to imagine what it might be like to be the woman in that dress. This is the basis for all human fascinations, and all reality television: desire and repulsion. In this show, I see a path not taken, much as I see a path not taken in the pageantry of the debutante. I do not want to be her, and yet I like watching her pick out her gloves.

By and large, women inherit their habits and neuroses about femininity from their mothers, and mine were inherited from my own Texan mother and, by extension, hers. The rituals of female beauty are deep-rooted in Texas, as is pageant culture—the desire to display the beauty of young women, and the sense that it is the moral duty of the mother to teach her daughter the rules of tasteful and advantageous self-presentation.

As a little girl I was carefully combed and dressed, with bows in my hair that matched my outfits. I went to cotillion with my friends—my brother did, too. I learned to fold my hands in my lap. I was enthusiastic about most of this, having been the kind of little girl who liked princesses and sparkly shoes. I enjoyed feeling pretty. I felt fancy eating crumbling grocery store cookies in white cotton gloves.

My mother is not the kind of woman who would enjoy *Say Yes to the Dress*, being both a self-proclaimed feminist and the person from whom I learned the devastating implications of the word "ostentatious." (She also taught me the word "gauche.") Her personal style was constructed as a rebuke to the big-hair-and-blue-eyeshadow stereotype of a Texas woman. Still, she is uncommonly beautiful—so much so that it's often the first quality of hers people remark upon—and she has stewarded that beauty vigilantly, in part because I think she understands appearance as a reflection of both character and aspiration, an occasion to demonstrate not just beauty but intelligence about who you are and where you belong. She has since told me that she wanted to equip me and my brother to move comfortably and inconspicuously through any kind of social space—that's why we went to cotillion. It was with that in mind that she dressed us as children.

As a teenager, I balked at learning to blow-dry my hair with a round brush or at being told not to go out without earrings. I argued, citing all the times she'd told me that what mattered most was my mind and character, saying that I shouldn't have to look pretty if I didn't want to, that how I looked wasn't the important thing about me. She argued that I should look "like I cared." She fought hard throughout my teen years to keep me from looking, in her estimation, "sloppy"—to keep me wearing clothing that was attractive and intentional but not overly alluring or sexual; to keep me wearing earrings every day; to keep me from leaving the house with wet or frizzy hair. In other words, she fought hard to keep me within the boundaries of how she felt young women should look and be, when I wasn't entirely sure that was what I wanted.

Still, there was a sliver of time when I might have been a debutante. I was twelve. We had moved to a new city in California, and in an attempt to make some friends, my mother let someone put her in touch with the local chapter of the National Charity League. My mother was skeptical about this from the beginning because, she said, societies like this were less about charity than about social climbing—a phrase that, because I was twelve, I needed her to define. Most mothers joined because they wanted to debut their daughters, which, she suggested, was a pretty antiquated and sexist ritual of declaring your daughter to be "on the market" to men. Nevertheless, she went ahead with our application, reasoning that she might be willing to deal with it if it would help us make friends in this new place.

The way I remember it, the meeting took place at some horse stables, and the girls were receiving a horse-riding lesson while the mothers chatted over tea. While I was bouncing around on top of a horse, my mother was being delicately grilled by the other mothers. As this story has been codified into our shared mother-daughter lore, this conversation was full of thinly veiled racism that took the form of skepticism about whether we were "the right kind of people." I've imagined the car ride on the way home, my mother's mouth set in a grim line.

When I called to ask my mother about this, she said she doesn't remember any meeting at all. She remembers a phone call with the mother in charge of the chapter, and that the questions on that call gave her the prickling feeling that having a last name like Garcia might be a stumbling block with the League ladies. The woman called her back a few days later and said they were refusing our application; there weren't enough people to vouch for us.

The evening before the pageant, between interviews and watching the dress rehearsal, I engaged in a dash around the Mall del Norte, looking for something, anything to wear to the ball. Poetically and idiotically, I'd come to Laredo without a gown of my own. As I was arriving in Laredo I talked briefly on the phone with the president of the Martha Washington Society, a woman named Minnie Dora Bunn. (Minnie is actually the fourth Minnie Dora Bunn; the original Minnie Dora Bunn was one of the charter members, and she and every subsequent Minnie Dora Bunn have served as Society president in their turn. The Minnie I spoke to, let's call her MDB4, recently gave birth to her first child, a girl, whose name surprised no one.) We chatted for only a few minutes about logistics before she asked, "Did you bring a dress?"

I froze. "I have a work dress that hits around the knee . . ."

"Is that all you have? You'll really need a floor-length formal dress," Minnie said, sounding sorry to break the news.

I confirmed with Tami. "Yeah, you need a long dress," she said, grinning. "And let's put it this way: It can't be too dressy. Don't think, It's too dressy. It's not."

The dress I found was full Vanna White glory: an ivory

boat-necked backless column dress sewn over completely with sequins. It itched, but it was light. It made me feel like I should give away a Volvo. I bought it.

I texted a picture of myself to my mother, telling her that I thought I might return it. As I did, I realized that it looked something like a wedding dress, if a slightly vampy one.

She texted me back. "It's stunning. Will you have an opportunity to wear it?" I decided I wouldn't.

They are breathtaking all together, and blinding. There are roughly a quarter of a million sequins and crystals catching the light. They look more like a squadron of ships than girls. Their traffic patterns are elaborate and cautious. The visual effect is reminiscent of aircraft carriers in a harbor. The disembodied voice of the emcee declares to the thousand people watching out there in the darkness, the mayor and his pretty wife, the Texas senators who have traveled to see them debut, that they are "the best of Laredo."

The stage of the Jesus Martinez Performing Arts Complex has been arranged with backdrops painted with bursting, fecund cherry trees surrounding a Palladian manor house: Mount Vernon. Three tiers of risers lead up to painted double doors, attended by two young pages, each outfitted in breeches and a false ponytail clipped into their crew cuts. Before any of the girls emerge at all, the bishop of the Diocese of Laredo prays over the event, and the Junior ROTC band plays the national anthem, and all one thousand audience members, dressed in their own best formal wear, rise and place hand over heart.

The most common form of pageantry in America is beauty competitions, but this show is a pageant more in the medieval or religious sense of the word. Medieval pageantry was like ritualized communal theater, put on seasonally or to celebrate particular saints' days. This kind of pageant has plot, elaborate costumes, and a rank assigned to each participant, denoted by their place in the procession. (Historically, the closer you were to the king, the higher your rank; here, it's about being close to George.) Medieval pageants held in honor of Corpus Christi reenacted the entire history of the world, starting with Genesis 1 and hauling all the way through to the Apocalypse. The 2018 Society of Martha Washington Colonial Pageant would reenact a fictional dinner party hosted by George and Martha in Mount Vernon with a party theme of, inexplicably, literacy.

They arrived one by one, in order of the status of their families within the Society. First came Andrea Victoria Gutierrez, daughter of Mr. and Mrs. Albert Gutierrez III. Andrea had been chosen to come first because her ancestral line within the Society is the longest and most distinguished, according to an elaborate and strictly maintained hierarchy: The girls with mothers who are members always come before girls who are related to the Society through another relative, and within each group the girls are ranked in order of the length of time the family has been in the Society. A girl whose mother is the first member in that family line, like Sydney, comes after all of these. If there are two girls with first-generation-member mothers, the girl whose mother joined first comes first. And so on.

Next come the girls whose connection to the Society is not a mother but another female relative, sub-ranked again in order of the date of membership. After this come two or three girls who have been invited as the Society's "guests" for the year. It's tradition to invite a girl from a neighboring city in Texas whose family has ties with the Society. It is also customary to invite a girl from Nuevo Laredo to debut with the Society. Any non-Laredoan Americans are presented after the Laredoan girls; the Mexican girl comes last.

This is the order in which their portraits appear in the yearbook-program, the order in which they are presented at the November father-daughter dance, the order of their names in the paper. In the citywide parade, at which each girl has her own corporate-sponsored float, blue-eyed Andrea Gutierrez's float will drive through first, at 9:30 a.m. Those farther back will wait their turn in the heat until finally Angela Moreno of Nuevo Laredo passes, sometime after noon.

I don't know what I had been imagining would happen during the pageant. Maybe a little play? Maybe elaborate choreography? Instead, when each girl was announced, as she appeared in the silhouette of the plywood double doors and began descending the stage, hand firmly gripping her escort for balance, the emcee read aloud an account of her breeding. Whether she was in boarding school or on honor roll, where she would be attending college, which prestigious activities she excelled at. More time and emphasis was devoted to who her mother was, who her father was, who their mothers and fathers and aunts and uncles were; what important positions, associations, or distinctions they enjoyed, as far back as possible. Two girls' bios made proud mention of genealogical connections to people who were involved in the Revolutionary War. One triumphantly traced her ancestry back to Patrick Henry, information that was received with excitement.

While her social stats were being announced, each girl walked a slow oval around the stage, smiling wide, moving carefully so that every angle of her could be admired. I understood, suddenly, why the girls had been so nervous about falling, wobbling, and tripping. The order of appearance identified the innate hierarchy, which was out of their hands, but each girl's promenade was her moment of evaluation before her community, much like the purebred's turn in the arena at Westminster. This slow-mo one-woman parade was her opportunity to be judged or celebrated for her beauty, grace, breeding, and accomplishment.

It was, finally, a display of wealth and a celebration of power through heredity, which is, in a sense, perfectly in line with the message of all classic debutante balls: Here is a girl who is someone, someone powerful and good. She is to be celebrated as an exemplar among young women, and the mechanism of her stature is that she comes from a family of stature. The older and more distinguished the family, the greater her glory.

All the members of the Society I spoke to were worried that I would portray this enterprise as elitist. They pointed out that anyone is welcome to apply for a membership in the Society of Martha Washington, and that in the past several years they've welcomed a number of new members who had no family ties to the organization. They pointed out as well that any woman, once a member, has the automatic right to present her daughter as a debutante when she is eighteen, and that conversely it's perfectly common and acceptable to not debut your eighteen-year-old.

It was important to them that I know that they are mostly working women. Nearly a dozen women I interviewed told me that the membership is full of "judges and doctors and lawyers and professors." The list was always the same: judges, doctors, lawyers, professors, indicating, I suppose, hardworking career-ism. "We are not the ladies that lunch," Tami summarized, over lunch. "There are very few ladies that lunch anymore."

Furthermore, they pointed out, the Society spends quite a bit of time and money on local philanthropy. They pay the fees for low-income Laredoan teenagers to go to a weeklong civic engagement program in Washington, D.C., every year. Their members sit on the boards of nonprofits, and privately raise money for charity throughout the year.

And furthermore, they argued, the pageant brings millions of dollars to the local economy. Out of their own pockets they pay hundreds of thousands of dollars to hairdressers and seam-stresses and cater waiters, jewelry designers and florists. The pageant effectively spreads their wealth.

Leaving aside the critique of trickle-down economics that notion might invite, it seemed what they were trying to insist is that though they may be wealthy and interested in exclusive memberships based around traditional definitions of "high so-ciety" as a group of people with special value (related to but not exactly synonymous with their special wealth), they're not unkind or unprincipled.

It is true that they were very kind. I wrote over and over again in my notebook that the women and girls (and orbiting young men) I interviewed were warm. They were skittish about having a reporter around because they felt they had been betrayed and misunderstood by other journalists who had painted them as frivolous elitists, but still they were welcoming. They seemed motivated by love of family, love of tradition, and love of country. They spoke over and over again about inclusivity, standing for unity with their "brothers and sisters in Nuevo Laredo." They mostly didn't speak the name of the president, but they often declared meaningfully that Laredoans believe in building bridges, not walls.

Neither did they seem to be rude about their wealth, unless you think public celebration of one's wealth and status is inherently rude—which, granted, some people do. The children were unfailingly polite and well-spoken. The mothers were anxious but reasonable. In general, they seemed to be a group of people aware of being on view, setting an example. They adhered, perhaps, to an old-fashioned notion of gentility.

I should admit here, in the interest of being fair, that these ideas about "society" don't appeal to me and so I am not inclined to agree with the premises of this spectacle. It may be true that the millions of dollars spent on the Colonial Pageant and Ball stimulate the local economy, and it may be true that the members of the Society do not intend to place themselves unpleasantly above the people who cannot participate, but it is also true that exclusivity is predicated on someone being excluded. It is also true that when you designate a group of young women to be the "best of Laredo," you are saying something about all the young women who have not managed to make their way into that glittering formation.

Throughout the pageant, I kept thinking of a moment from earlier in the day in the makeup salon, after Tami left. I was hanging around chatting with a makeup artist while she did another debutante's makeup, and she told me that years ago, when she was first starting to do makeup for the pageants, the hardest thing for her was remembering that the girls in the Society have different coloring.

"Most people in the Society are lighter?"

"Yes," she said. "Most are. Or they have European blood in them. And that's what it is, the pageant. They're telling you all their lineage, and that's European blood." She smiled a little smile. "I call them Martians. Because they look good in greens."

I asked about the other pageant that happens this time of year, the Princess Pocahontas Pageant. It started around the same time as the Colonial Pageant and Ball, but carries on honoring Pocahontas's original role in the festivities. As it's described on the website, this pageant celebrates the "regal Indian maiden" and "presents the Native Americans in a setting that is both mystical and natural." I wondered aloud whether the girls who played Pocahontas and her court were also Martians.

She shook her head. "No. The Society is . . . the crème de la crème, so to speak. It's—you're born into that."

She told me that this year, Tami invited her to one of her parties for the Society. "Tami is so down to earth, and so nice," she said. "But are you kidding me!? I don't have anything to wear, I don't even know what to wear. I shop at Target and Walmart, and there's just no way I can be there and feel comfortable." She shook her head, her expression somewhere between laughter and a grimace. "You realize, Oh, wow, there's a really different world out there. It's not my world."

I recalled this as I watched one winsome young woman after

another arrive on the stage and float down the stairs to applause. This is your world, their community was telling Andrea Gutierrez and Bianca Martinez and Jordan Puig and Rebecca Peterson and Rebecca Reyes and Lauren Moore and Azul Martinez and Leticia Garcia and Marissa Gonzalez, and all the rest. This whole beautiful world is for you.

My mother called one afternoon, a few months after I left Laredo and went back to New York. "Hey babes," she said.

"Hi mom," I said.

"What are you doing?" she said. I told her I was trying to write the Laredo essay, as I'd been trying to write it for months now, and that I was having a hard time. I'd wind up in tears at my inadequacy in the face of this subject, though to what I was inadequate I couldn't quite say. I knew my scenes: salon, pageant, border. I knew history and theory. I knew my intellectual issues: the paradox of a borderlands George Washington celebration, respectability politics, assimilation and class anxiety, the need to be American that seems to grow stronger and stronger the closer you get to the border.

I had it all in my mind, and still I experienced that feeling of inability every time I sat down to write, a panic more precise than writer's block, more a failure of ethics than of imagination or creativity.

"Why?" she asked.

And then I realized that my problem had a very simple, if powerful, cause. I had undertaken this story not out of journalistic curiosity but because I saw in the pageant echoes of a force in my own family that I wanted to understand. I didn't know how to write about this story without writing about what it means to my family, and I didn't want to do that to my mother. My mother, whose name I haven't yet included in this essay. Her name is Carmen Rosette Garcia, though she has always, from the day she was born, been called Rosette.

Somewhere along the way I came to believe that to write about the complexity of who my mother is—the family she was born into, and who she chose to become—would constitute a betrayal. It was from my mother's family, my mother's Mexican American Catholic military family, born out of the poverty of the Rio Grande Valley, that I learned to be a person who can fit in anywhere because she seems to come from nowhere, a person without mythology other than the one she is making herself, right now. An American.

I started to tell her, in my own stumbling way, that I was grappling with how the pressure to be American that's so extreme in these Texan hinterlands was brought to bear on our family. I recognized in Laredo a dynamic I'd seen play out before: an equation of Americanness with middle-class whiteness that's exerted so powerfully on brown people that they eventually begin to accede and conform.

Then my mother started to tell me things she'd never told me outright so much as implied. She told me about the South Texas my grandmother grew up in, where there were laws against speaking Spanish in public school, and how my grandmother was punished as a child for speaking Spanish on the playground even though it was her first language. She told me about the separate drinking fountains. She told me that in

Mission, the train tracks really were the dividing line between the white neighborhood and the Mexican neighborhood, and that the roads on the Mexican side went unpaved until the late seventies.

She told me that Mission has a pageant, too, the Mission Texas Citrus Fiesta. Mission is one of the biggest producers of citrus in the country, specifically Ruby Red grapefruits, and her grandfather was a foreman for one of the citrus producers. When she was five years old, my grandmother entered my mother—the firstborn daughter—into a contest to select the Court of Queen Citrianna. "I didn't even know what I was doing, I had to learn to curtsy and all that. It was probably the blond girls who were selected." She made a sound between a laugh and a sigh and I could see her in my mind's eye, shaking her head on the other end of the phone. "My mother came from a really nothing family, right, but she had these aspirations."

She told me things I'd heard before but never so succinctly: that at home her parents chose not to speak Spanish so that their children would learn only English, and that her mother would punish them if their words ever took on the melodic singsong intonation of Spanglish from the Valley. "*Do not speak like that*," she said, imitating my grandmother's voice, which is itself accented. "*You're going to sound like you're Mexican.*" "There was nothing to be gained by being Latino or bilingual," she said. "As Mexican Americans you pretty much wanted to subsume your racial identity. And there was no 'Mexican-American' when I was growing up! You didn't hyphenate. You lost that. You were just American."

Because my grandfather was in the military, my grandparents

left the Rio Grande Valley soon after they were married, and raised their children traveling between San Antonio and far-flung military bases throughout the United States and in Italy and Turkey, where they lived mostly among white people. It seemed important to my grandmother to fit in these spaces, and for her children not to seem too Mexican, too from-the-Valley. "But how did she draw that line?" I interrupted, asking a question I'd been wanting to ask for years. "It's like she saw a line between her kind of Mexican and another, worse kind. Where's the line?"

My mother laughed in a rueful, painful way. "The lines are with those who are too Mexican. Who haven't done their best to become American. Who haven't taken on all the WASP white-America values and looks and aspirations. People who are just too invested in their own ethnicity."

All of my grandmother's seven children married white people. None of her grandchildren speaks fluent Spanish. My grandfather made a career in the U.S. Army, as did one of my uncles and several of my cousins and cousins' husbands, which is a source of great pride and patriotism in our family. No family is more American than a military family, the logic goes. Everyone who had an opportunity to change their last name through marriage did, with the sole exception of my mother. The parts of the family history that held poverty or immigration or the "wrong" kind of Mexicanness or any other perceived stain were dropped from conversation so that my generation would never know them.

But why? I'd always wanted to know. This was all totally antithetical to the kind of pro-multicultural America I was told I lived in as I was growing up. When I asked my mother, she was quick to point out that in the areas where she grew up, Mexicans and the indigenous people who preceded them were enslaved. In the roughly thirty years between the founding of the WBCA and my grandparents' birth, Texas rangers tortured and executed Mexicans down in the borderlands en masse. A Texas newspaper defended the killings as a reasonable response to "a serious surplus population that needs eliminating." Prominent Texas politicians were calling for "all those of Mexican descent" to be sent to concentration camps.

My grandparents grew up in that place, a geographically and culturally marginal part of the country that was desperately economically depressed. My grandmother in particular was raised in poverty, and though my grandparents came to speak English fluently, it was a second language. Neither of them went to college—though my grandfather went to flight school and became a highly trained pilot, in part to facilitate getting up and out of Mission. In the decades between their coming of age and mine, American politics has developed new language for people who fit my grandmother's description in the moment when she was making decisions about who and how to be. We call them vulnerable populations. What would a refusal or failure to assimilate have cost her?

In the months after I visited Laredo, the news broke that the U.S. government had begun separating migrant children from their parents at the Mexican border. Between May and June, two thousand children were taken from their families and put into detention centers, and by July new outlets were estimating that nearly twelve thousand immigrant children were in U.S.

custody. Several thousand were in a new tent camp in the desert outside El Paso. The youngest children, many of them still infants, some of them taken away from their mothers as they were breastfeeding, were sent to "tender-age" shelters in South Texas. Laredo's detention center, which is about seven miles northeast of the bridge where the Abrazo ceremony takes place, mostly holds parents, but in McAllen, the city next door to Mission, which was widely credited as the epicenter of family separation policy, the press released photos of children being held in cages. Some were sent to foster homes and put up for adoption as wards of the state. Their parents, meanwhile, were being deported back to their home countries without being told where their children were. "They treated us as though we were animals," wrote one woman in a letter to her lawyer. In August 2019, a man massacred twenty-two people in a Walmart in El Paso after publishing a manifesto online that explained, "This attack is in response to the Hispanic invasion of Texas."

It was shocking but not entirely surprising, since the president ran on building a wall to "keep out the Mexicans"—which is the standard nomenclature for anyone south of the border. "They're bringing drugs," he claimed during his campaign. "They're bringing crime. They're rapists." In 2015, someone uncovered a mass grave of immigrants who'd been dumped in the desert in Falfurrias, ninety miles east of Laredo. The same year, Texas officials were denying birth certificates to children whose mothers lacked visas, in defiance of the Constitution.

Writing about the particular ferocity of anti-Mexican racism and violence on the border, the historian Greg Grandin suggests that the border is where so-called white Americans have felt literally marginalized, most vulnerable to becoming the "other" they fear. If borders signify "domination and exploitation," he writes, "they also announce the panic of power, something that overcomes a political state similar to the way dread comes over an individual with the realization that their psyche isn't theirs to control alone, that it's formed in reaction to others." He quotes Freud: "The phobia is thrown before the anxiety like a fortress on the frontier."

I'd always had the sense, formed subliminally or even innately, that it was better to erase the past. My grandmother carried and then pushed her children as far as possible from her upbringing toward an imagined ideal of power, affluence, respectability, and credibility. And my mother, in turn, carried and pushed me as far from her own upbringing as she could, clear across the country to California, then to the Ivy League and then to New York, to this life I lead now.

In ways I don't like to contemplate, my life as an excellently educated, widely traveled, white-passing American woman was the dream behind that erasure. What could be more ungrateful than to redraw in public what was so carefully and privately elided?

Still, my mother took steps to preserve the parts of her that her mother wanted gone. She intentionally learned Spanish in her youth, and began, in the eighties, referring to herself as Mexican American. "That's very much the reason why I didn't change my name when I got married," she said. After a beat, she added, "Though going to Rosette Kisner would have been the ultimate success, in a way."

When people inquire after my mother's ethnicity she tells

them now that she's "as Mexican as you can get" because her father was a Garcia and her mother is a Martinez, which, she always adds, is like the Smith and Jones of the Mexican world. "Both my parents are Mexican and *completely* Mexican," she says.

I'd been sort of puzzled by the emphasis, particularly because it's not categorically true: the most Mexican you can get, in one sense, is to be from Mexico. This gets at a key—if confusing—element of the second- or third-generation Mexican American experience: your Mexican-ness isn't always constructed based on your relationship to Mexico as a country. When I asked her about it she said, "I feel like I have to sort of convince people that I'm Mexican. I don't feel Mexican enough." Where she and my father live in San Diego (north county, near the coast), most of their social spaces are white, and it bothers her that her features are ambiguous enough that her whole life people have been asking her "where she's from."

This shouldn't have surprised me, but it did. My mother is often the yardstick by which I estimate myself, and I had always assumed that I didn't feel Mexican enough because I was not enough like her. When I was growing up she used to tell a story about how she and my father moved to Paris shortly after they were married, and when I was born she began to take me to the park near our apartment in an affluent neighborhood. Most of the women at the park during the day were foreign au pairs tending to the babies of the white women who lived nearby. I was a fair baby with gold hair; my mother was mistaken for my au pair.

I always heard this story as an example of racial bias: my

mother, a young, olive-skinned woman, was assumed to be the help rather than the mother. I also noted it as the first time that I was "not Mexican enough" to be recognizable. Subliminally, I understood it as a story about the deepest form of intergenerational betrayal: a daughter who doesn't resemble her mother. It strikes me now that my mother might not have thought of it that way at all—that she might have just felt lonely in the park, caught between the mothers and the au pairs.

In Nahuatl, there's a word for in-betweenness: *nepantla*. The Aztecs started using the word in the sixteenth century when they were being colonized by Spain. *Nepantla* meant in the middle, which is what they were: between a past they wrote and the future that would be written by their conquerors, in the middle of the river between who they had been and who they were allowed to be now. Twentieth-century theorists have used the word "shattered" to describe the liminal existence of *nepantleras*, indicating both brokenness and the possibility of making something radically new. The word has been used to describe the borderlands experience, the mixed-race experience, the experience of anyone who lives both in and outside their world of origin. As Gloria Anzaldúa wrote, *nepantleras* are "threshold people."

I hesitate to draw parallels between my life and my mother's because they are not the same life—by her design. My mother raised me with the hope that she could be my threshold, that her sacrifices and mistakes, her proximity to oppression, would deliver me to a different life, a life of being inside, where there was no space I wouldn't occupy comfortably, wherein the whole beautiful world was for me. But I am *nepantla* in my ways, too. I, too, know what it feels like to pass without exactly wanting to.

It does not seem like a coincidence that a pageant devoted to celebrating a Eurocentric story about the American project should involve corsets and false eyelashes and elaborate, perfectly uniform curtsies—given that modern pageantry is a kissing cousin to drag, or given that sites of extreme pressure to conform racially or nationally tend to beget even greater pressure to conform along lines of gender and sex. The pageant girl reflects an ideal that's being championed: wealth, national pride, a precise if exaggerated performance of traditional femininity, young beauty on the arm of a man. All that is in the dress.

In my twenties, in the years when I'd begun seeing women but hadn't yet told my mother about it, our disagreements over my clothing got worse, as my wardrobe migrated toward grays and tans, loose shapes, long necklaces, and clunky boots. There were minor tussles whenever I was home and tried to leave the house without earrings. I recall thinking that she looked at my clothing with distrust. I was becoming a different kind of woman than she is, and though I've never asked her about it, I think she could sense it from the cut of my shirts.

When I told my mother, finally, that I was in love with a woman, she was shocked and not a little outraged. I had always dated men, she reminded me. I'd been with one man for five whole years. Had I just been lying my way through that?

No, I tried to explain. I was attracted to men and women. I was choosing to be with women. I was in love with this woman.

"Don't," she said. "Just don't." She couldn't understand why, if I could be straight, if I could be safely inside the majority, I'd choose to be outside. Furthermore, she couldn't understand why if I wasn't going to be straight, I couldn't just go ahead and be gay—why I was insisting that I was some kind of in-between thing.

I was angry about this conversation for a long time. It wasn't until later that I realized that she may have been ex-pressing the kind of fear that comes from experience—it's not an easy thing to live as not quite one thing and not quite an-other when it's not a circumstance you have chosen. What I didn't then have language to tell her is that if you are lucky enough to be able to choose, if someone has seen to it that you are safe enough to choose, it can feel like freedom.

Once or twice, I tried to explain to my mother the feeling I had when I was watching the Marthas onstage. Even though I saw the forces of what constrained her and her mother and her mother's mother, even though I saw the corsets and the money and the bald desire to fit into a jingoistic idea of Americanness that contorts the people it touches—even though I saw all that, it also made my stomach flip. Because there was bilingual Leti-cia Garcia, "daughter of Mr. and Mrs. Hector Garcia," beaming before a thousand people while the names of her parents and grandparents were read as honorifics. You can say that it was sim-ply because her family had money and that this is just a contin-uation of the pathological "right kind of Mexican" self-policing, and you'd be right. I'd just never gotten to see a girl named Garcia from South Texas stand in front of a room of the most powerful people in government and society and be celebrated specifically for her "excellent" lineage. It was like seeing an alternate history. And I was ashamed, but I was moved.

The morning after the pageant, I woke up early and drove down to the Juarez-Lincoln International Bridge to see the Abrazo ceremony. George Washington, an affable guy named Tim, had assured me that I could park downtown by the historic San Agustin Plaza and then walk the two blocks to the bridge.

Coming into Laredo near the main border crossing, you see first the mostly abandoned colonial structures of the old city: a tiled plaza rimmed with stylish Spanish stucco buildings that now lie mostly empty. The library was abandoned and emptied decades ago, and aside from a boutique hotel fashioned out of one of the renovated colonial buildings and the San Agustin Cathedral, which still holds Mass in Spanish, the historic downtown has a derelict quiet about it.

The streets downtown were empty. I parked near an abandoned office building and walked the few blocks of uneven pavement to the bridge entrance only to find it, too, empty except for three ICE officers hanging around near their booths. Juarez-Lincoln isn't a pedestrian bridge, it's a five-lane highway, so I hopped a little gate and walked the quiet pavement toward the officers.

"I'm trying to see the Abrazo," I said.

The young man squinted at me. "Who are you? Are you with the mayor's office?"

When I explained, he shook his head. "The Abrazo ceremony isn't open to the public."

I'd believed, based on the way that everyone from the Society had talked about the Abrazo, that it was a moment of mutual public celebration. I'd foolishly imagined that Laredoans would walk onto the bridge from the north side and Nuevo Laredoans would walk out onto the south side, and they would meet in the middle. I'd pictured the two cities behaving as one city, the bridge open, cheers and music as the children hugged.

But there was nothing to see from the American side except the implacable faces of the ICE officers, and nothing to hear at all. Of course the bridge is never left wide open in Laredo to whoever wants to cross, not even on this day. The children are escorted out by the mayors and city officials, their parents, ICE officers, and military from both sides. A dais is set up in the middle of the bridge, garlanded in red, white, and blue, and the children are called forth by a dignitary. They approach each other, the four of them alone on the road. The little girl from Laredo is dressed like a mini Martha, the little boy like George. The children from Nuevo Laredo are dressed as was fashionable during the Spanish colonial period, with the girl in a mantilla and the boy in a sombrero, and each girl hugs the boy across from her.

I listened to it on the radio in my rental car. As I drove back north, the city still seemed to be sleeping.

By the time I arrived near the parade grounds, it had woken. It's hard to explain the mood of a town on the morning of an event like this: Every elevator held a man carrying a ruffled shirt in a garment bag. There were squads of kids in dance costumes camped out on the floor of my hotel lobby. Outside, ball-capped fathers had staked out positions on the bleachers with umbrellas and thick coolers full of beer and snacks.

The Anheuser-Busch Washington's Birthday Parade is for the whole city, and everyone from the local children's dance studio to H-E-B supermarket employees—riding a fourteen-foot-tall grocery cart—participates. In between them all, paced every five floats, are the dresses on parade, each with a girl inside it, each dress and its girl on their own corporate-sponsored parade float.

It is customary at this parade for the girls to have attendants ride with them on their floats and throw little gifts to the crowd. It is also customary for the people standing on the parade's sidelines, catching the trinkets, to shout for the girls to lift up their heavy skirts and show their shoes. *Muéstranos tus zapatos!* This seems like an almost philosophical response to spectacle: an audience looking at young women in a state of exquisite display, corseted and contoured, fake hair piled high, and demanding to see what they're hiding.

Up comes the manteau, the petticoats, the hoop, and when everyone sees what's underneath, they cheer.

This is the moment that former debs talk about as the fondest memory, the part where the whole city gets to see and admire the dresses. For most of them it will be the only time in their lives that this many people will look at them all at once and applaud.

In *Say Yes to the Dress*, the moment always comes when,

after trying on and discarding dozens of gowns, the woman approaches the mirror in The One. This is the denouement of the episode, and it's always the same. She steps up onto the pedestal in the showroom, sees her reflection, and is bewitched, thrilled, her own dream of herself coming true. Her mother, who perhaps has had reservations about some of the other options, immediately weeps. The air molecules in the room speed up.

"Are you saying yes to this dress?" Randy asks.

Through tears, the woman nods. "Yes," she whispers, or shouts, or sobs. "Yes!" Everyone cheers, even the bitchy sister. This, in the logic of the show, is the happy ending. (The wedding, if they show it in the closing credits, is simply the occasion where she displays this achievement.)

So American, this show; you just go to the store and choose yourself off a rack at your preferred price point. As a metaphor—only as a metaphor—the Marthas' dresses are so much more realistic: your mother or your sister or an aunt hands you a hundred-pound corseted structure and says, Walk in that, and then you make a lot of decisions about what of the gown you want to keep, whether you'll change its color, cut off the weird embellishments the last wearer put on, add a whole new panel, or change everything about it except its bones, which cannot change.

I stayed at the parade for a while, weaving between the children jumping for beads and the fathers in lawn chairs who'd rise and angrily tap the shoulder of any passersby who paused and blocked their view. Marching bands and baton twirlers sandwiched the local Catholic bishop, who was riding on the back of a convertible like a teenager. Princess Pocahontas and her court, dressed in giant feathered headdresses and ornately beaded suede, rode skittering horses to great applause. ICE had a large formation of armored vehicles.

The last girl I saw for the day was Sydney, who, despite the pain the dress was causing her, was beaming and waving. She wants to be a lawyer when she grows up. You could hardly tell she was sitting on a stool until the crowd yelled for her to show them her shoes. She smiled obligingly, gathered her skirts in each hand, heaved them upward, and kicked. There was a swirl of color: the peach and lavender of her dress reared back, revealing petticoats and then a splash of sequins. She was wearing six-inch platform go-go boots with another five inches of heel, covered toe-to-knee in sequins. Custom made and star-spangled, red, white, and blue.

An appreciative roar went through the crowd. When Sydney saw me, I gave her a wave, and then turned and began the walk back to my hotel, kicking the confetti in the dirt.

STITCHING

Naomi Davis lives on Manhattan's Upper West Side, and when the weather is warm she likes to walk around the city for miles at a time wearing a fashionable hat and taking pictures. She has eyelash extensions, and her favorite lipstick, the one she wears "like it's ChapStick," is Maybelline's Pink Me Up. She loves doughnuts from the Doughnut Plant in Chelsea and cupcakes from Georgetown Cupcake, but replaces them with green smoothies when her husband Josh convinces her to give up added sugar. She danced at ABT as a teenager and then later at Juilliard, then married Josh, who attended Columbia. She stopped dancing to raise their five children: Eleanor, Samson, Conrad, Madalena, and Beatrice. For a while, Eleanor wanted to be an astronaut when she grew up. Conrad dressed as a spider for Halloween.

I've never met these people, but still I can recite these facts more or less on command—alongside the names of Naomi's siblings, her preferred pizza restaurant in Washington, D.C., the store where she got the couch in her living room, the symptoms of her last pregnancy, and a series of other personal details I can't confidently say I know about my closest friends—because I have been reading Naomi's blog since I was twenty-one and she was twenty-four.

Naomi is widely agreed to be the queen of "The Bloggernacle," a contingent of Mormon mothers who have taken over a sizable piece of the online aspirational-lifestyle industry. There have been many taxonomies of what's sometimes derisively called the "Mormon mommy blog," and Naomi's, *Love Taza*, is frequently the benchmark. Many of these blogs began as a way for stay-at-home wives and mothers to pass the time and to keep in touch with family. As a genre they offer a portrait of the domestic woman that looks stimulating and joyous. The Davis family often gathers to sing raucously around the canary-yellow piano in their living room, and at Christmas they wear matching green-and-red-striped pajamas. In the fall, they wrap up in fuzzy coats and traipse downtown for a slice of pizza in the West Village, and in the summer they try out all the playgrounds and Popsicles in Manhattan. They take trips to Europe, where they dance on mountaintops in the Alps, circled by airborne drone cameras that get jaw-dropping 360-degree footage. This all looks, on its face, like an advertisement for the traditional family values held dear by the Mormon church: Father wearing a bow tie, Mother in a pretty skirt with a backpack full of snacks, a whole bunch of smiling, freckled babies, and everyone laughing together. It's remarkably beautiful.

Quietly over the last ten years, *Love Taza* and other sites like it have evolved into something resembling miniature advertising empires. In 2010, Naomi Davis was a stay-at-home mother who occasionally volunteered teaching ballet to toddlers; Josh was supporting the family by working in finance. Four years later, Josh quit a VP position at Bank of America to work for his wife; in 2017, *Forbes* named Naomi among the top-ten influencers in parenting. The same year, a writer from *The Atlantic* suggested that the most successful Mormon lifestyle bloggers, *Love Taza* among them, generate up to six million dollars annually in corporate partnerships and advertising. Over time, both Davises have become skilled lifestyle photographers, and Naomi, who is exceptionally beautiful, is a ready model for brands ranging from Kate Spade to Band-Aid to the City of New Orleans tourism office.

The message the blog conveys through Naomi's photos and brief lowercase missives remains the same: her children, she constantly reminds us, "are the most important, most prized and special and beautiful things i have in my life. they are what matter most for me, and everything else is absolutely second." Nevertheless, she and other bloggers like her—Amber Fillerup Clark of *Barefoot Blonde* and Jordan Ferney of *Oh Happy Day!* are two especially powerful digital Mormons—are some of the most valuable "influencers" online, with followings so large and devoted that brands like Target and Citibank will pay top dollar to include their products in a post.

This has all been happening at the same time that an argument has erupted within the Church of Latter-Day Saints about how women should be spending their time, and, to put it bluntly, what exactly women are for. Mormon women often insist that they are neither oppressed nor repressed by the patriarchal structure of their faith and its attendant culture; still, in the last five years, they have slowly begun to push for more power. A subset of the Bloggernacle arose that was explicitly feminist: *Feminist Mormon Housewives*, *The Exponent*, a literary journal and blog called *Segullah*, and dozens more. A human rights attorney named Kate Kelly founded an organization called Ordain Women, arguing that women should be permitted to join the LDS priesthood, for which she was formally excommunicated from the church in 2015. Others founded Aspiring Mormon Women, a group intended to encourage Mormon women to pursue higher education and careers. Books like *Mormon Feminism: Essential Writings* hit the market, and the church itself published a history of the early years of their women's organization, emphasizing the LDS belief in a Heavenly Mother.

Love Taza, like its lifestyle-blog peers, remains starkly apolitical in tone. With vanishingly few exceptions, its sunny online space depicts a world in which there are no elections, no movements, nothing really that might appear in a newspaper. But this is the strangeness of the internet: Naomi's lipstick tips led me to Kate Kelly, who led me to a woman named Sharlee Mullins Glenn, which is how I wound up having lunch with a group of lovely Mormon women who bake brownies and sew their many children's Halloween costumes and would like nothing more than to politely overthrow the government.

Sharlee Mullins Glenn is a pert and pretty children's book author in her early sixties, with wispy bangs, wide eyes, and a high, sweet voice. She has a certain demureness in her manner that's easy to misinterpret as diffidence. Actually, her personality runs more toward ferocity, in a maternal sort of way. Once, walking through a Renaissance fair, she saw a tall, heavyset teenager beating up a smaller kid, and she marched over and spanked him like a toddler. "I spanked his bottom! I did!" As her husband likes to say, Let this indicate the mettle of the woman.

In 2017, Sharlee quietly and accidentally became one of the most influential Mormon women in the world. She is the reluctant leader of a movement called Mormon Women for Ethical Government, a group of more than five thousand Mormon women who have banded together to fight Trump's policies and corrupt government wherever they see it. When I asked her what her personal feelings were toward Trump, she gritted her teeth. "I want to spank him!"

The week of Trump's inauguration, Sharlee and a group of writer friends were trading despondent emails about his first days in office: the appointments, the travel ban, the birth of "alternative facts." These women had been among the 49 percent of Mormons who, for the first time, divided the Mormon vote, which has been unanimously conservative for decades. Only

61 percent of Mormons voted for Trump; the rest voted for Hillary Clinton or Evan McMullin, the Utah-born Mormon who became a last-minute independent candidate. Mormon women in particular disdained Trump throughout the election cycle on the grounds that he was as un-Mormon a candidate as had ever crossed the national stage: dishonest, vulgar, misogynistic, avaricious, xenophobic, and so on. This is everything their church preaches against, they say.

When Trump took office, they were horrified to learn that he was as good as his word. "It was like, My gosh, he's doing everything he said he would do," Sharlee said. "And I thought, We need to strategize, we need to organize, we need to mobilize, so let's get together and figure out how to do that." She stayed up until two in the morning setting up a secret Facebook group where her friends could concentrate their conversations about resistance, named it "Mormon Women for Ethical Government" because that seemed to the point, invited twenty-five writer friends, and went to bed.

When she woke up, there were more than twenty-five members. In the first three days, over three hundred women joined. After two weeks, the secret MWEG group on Facebook had ballooned to more than four thousand. Dozens of women were being added to the group by the hour, each with her own agenda. (Several MWEG members claimed to me that, contrary to public perception, the swath of the American West they call "the Mormon corridor" is a fairly accurate reflection of the whole country's political and economic demographics.) Some of the women joining MWEG's Facebook forum were lifelong Republicans, others were proud socialists; some hated Trump because of his immigration policies but were perfectly happy to have an anti-gay agenda in the White House while others were furious about incursions on LGBTQ rights but wanted to "build the wall." Everyone was angry about the election.

When I spoke to Sharlee over the phone, the day MWEG's official website launched, she sounded a little breathless. "We never saw ourselves as activists, but my goodness!" She laughed. She'd been up most of the last several nights trying to get everything organized.

"The best analogy that I've come up with is that a little group of friends thought we were going out for a little rowboat ride on a Sunday afternoon, and suddenly four thousand women jump in the boat." She suggested I come see the mass mobilization for myself. "Because the thing that's so fascinating is—what does this tell us about what's going on with Mormon women?"

"Well, right," I said.

I met Sharlee in one of the strip malls that string together Salt Lake City's infrastructure. She and her husband, Jim, had invited me for Thai food at one of their favorite places, and when I arrived they rose with shining, gracious smiles and told me that they'd already ordered their favorite thing on the menu: a giant bowl of tom yum soup for sharing. "It's really quite excellent," Sharlee assured me.

We had only an hour before she had to make an appearance at an event at a local mosque, so she gave me the history of Mormon Women for Ethical Government quickly. After the

Facebook group ballooned to several thousand women, Sharlee and the other six cofounders threw together a brief statement of purpose, declaring themselves to be "a nonpartisan group dedicated to the ideals of decency, honor, accountability, transparency, and justice in governing."

MWEG's initiatives have been driven by happenstance. Many members were infuriated by the Utah congressman Jason Chaffetz, who had denounced Trump after the *Access Hollywood* tapes went public and then reversed course a few days before the election. As the chairman of the House Committee on Oversight and Government Reform, he was now refraining from investigating Trump's potential ethical violations. Incensed, MWEG authored an op-ed in *Deseret News*, the oldest paper in the state, and blasted his office with dozens of calls a day.

In May 2017, MWEG members sent rafts of "get well" cards in purple envelopes to Chaffetz's home daily, sweetly wishing him a swift recovery from minor foot surgery so that he could go do his job and investigate Trump. In the internal memo circulated for "Operation Purple Rain," as the project was called, members were encouraged to "marinate in the principles of Gandhi, Martin Luther King Jr. and Jesus" and to "make sure the tone of your messages is in the sweet spot between a bunch of Mormon ladies writing him love notes and a bunch of 'paid protestors' rudely invading his privacy to push their own political agendas." They were enthusiastic, but never got to finish the "Operation": the congressman announced his resignation.

"There are all kinds of people doing whatever they can to do good in the world, but one of the strengths we have is our commitment to civil discourse," Sharlee told me. She thumped the table gently with her fist. "We are brothers and sisters here on this fragile planet. How are we going to understand each other?"

Before this year, Sharlee had no experience with activism, beyond posting pro-Hillary material on her Facebook page and mentioning that she's a feminist to her neighbors, which is considered outré in her neighborhood. "'Feminism' is still a dirty word among most members of the church," she said, pursing her lips.

The next afternoon I drove out to a strip mall near the Museum of Ancient Life in Lehi, Utah, to meet with two young MWEG members named Mandee and Kristin, who'd recently discovered the history of Mormon women as campaigners and suffragists. Both were mothers in their mid-thirties and life-long Republicans who had nevertheless voted for Hillary Clinton and felt crushed when she lost. We'd arranged to meet at a restaurant in the back corner of the mall. As soon as we started talking, they brought up the Mormon suffragette Emmeline Wells, who campaigned with Elizabeth Cady Stanton and Susan B. Anthony. Mormons don't often talk about that time in history, they told me, but learning that there were Mormon proto-feminists had felt like a revelation to each of them.

The modern LDS church in which they grew up frames gender relations around a strict but—ideally—benevolent patriarchy. For a period beginning in the 1960s and '70s there was an emphasis in the church on women rejecting the "cult of individuality," their term for the increasingly mainstream women's lib notion that women should be fulfilled in themselves. This, the church taught, was a dangerous idea, and a grave threat to children and the family.

Though it varies by ward, or congregation, this attitude persists. Women are revered as givers of life, as caretakers of the young, as nurturers of families. They are regularly given authority over children and other women, and are put in charge of Sunday school classes, charity work, and educational and social organizations. There's even a Heavenly Mother, just like there's a Heavenly Father. Mandee and Kristin, like every woman I met in the Salt Lake area, were college-educated.

But women interested in exploring outside their "eternal" roles of maternal and wifely duties remain suspect. "One of the barriers in Utah or amongst Mormons are the two words 'career' and 'job,'" Mandee said, twisting her mouth. "It's okay to get a job, but as soon as you talk about having a career, that's when things get a little uncomfortable. I don't know why." She fought to keep working part-time from home, an effort she's felt confident to make only because she'd worked as a young woman and married "a little late," at twenty-four.

Both women—in fact, all the MWEG members I spoke to—were quick to point out that the degree of patriarchy or sexism faced by Mormon women depends on the location and culture of their home ward. They reassured me that most LDS men had their hearts in the right place, that some of their husbands identified as feminists, and that for many Mormon women, abstaining from politics or public leadership is their preference.

But when Trump was elected, another MWEG member

told me, "a lot of women realized that they'd thought, Politics is not for me, politics doesn't affect me, I'll just let other people who know do it, and then they realized what happens when we allow other people to make decisions for us."

"Do you mean men?" I asked.

"Engaged people," she said. "Yes, men, honestly."

For many members, stumbling across Mormon Women for Ethical Government online felt like finding a tribe. *I didn't know there were so many other women who felt this way*, ran many of the early comments.

I suspect they wouldn't like me to say so, because there are Mormon women the world over fighting this stereotype, but talking to them felt like time travel. It was like being granted an opportunity to speak to my mother in the late seventies, when she was being told that women didn't major in the sciences, or that if she worked really hard she could be a dentist's secretary someday. As a woman raised in California by and among people who believed in women's power and equality, I have always understood that my attitude toward gender isn't universal. Of course I knew that there are many people who think "feminism" is a nasty word used by ugly women. Of course I knew that broader American culture still systemically victimizes women, whether by undermining their professional success, legislating against their medical care, or insisting that they have to be half-naked to be on a magazine cover. I've talked to misogynistic people in Michigan and Los Angeles and the Dairy Queens in southern Louisiana, and I've been sexually harassed by both a corporate boss and a college professor; I've fended off assault from men I know and been roofied by one I didn't; I've been choked in a public place by the descendant of not one but two American presidents, and seen firsthand many ways that people lash back against the notion that women deserve to be powerful and free. But honest to God, I'd never before been to a place in the United States where the women's movement just never happened.

They are making it again, almost as if from scratch. "I get pushback in my ward from people who think I'm going to hell," one member told me. Another heard a man in her ward mutter, "No way there are five thousand women who feel this way."

In late April 2017, Sharlee received a frantic call from a woman in her church saying that a Mexican American woman named Silvia Avelar-Flores had been seized by ICE in nearby Salt Lake City. Avelar-Flores had been shopping for birthday party supplies with her seven-year-old daughter when she was arrested and driven hours to a holding facility to await deportation. Brought into the country illegally as a young child, Avelar-Flores had applied for legal status, consistently complied with regulations for undocumented immigrants, and recently been issued a work permit. She was the mother of three, the youngest still a toddler.

Immediately, Sharlee called Avelar-Flores's husband. Because of its own history—fleeing Illinois and Missouri in the mid-1800s, migrating west, remaining somewhat outside of mainstream American culture—the Mormon church in recent years has urged its members to advocate for refugees and immigrants. Sharlee's first action was to locate Avelar-Flores's work permit, which ICE had issued. Other members reached out to the ACLU and the local chapter of Indivisible, the nation-wide resistance network that had sprung up after the election. Groups of Mormon women with babies in tow organized a sit-in at ICE offices, where they sang worship songs.

Sharlee tracked down Senator Orrin Hatch's director of constituent services, a woman named Sharon Garn, who she'd heard could persuade the senator to stay the deportation and review the case. Sharlee put Garn on her speed-dial, calling her almost hourly. "You are the only person in this state who can save this family," Sharlee told her. "We are calling on you to save this family. Five thousand Mormon women are praying right now for you to do what you need to do."

Although Mormon women are often stereotyped as "subser-vient doormats," as one MWEG member put it, they are also afforded great deference in Utah, because they are associated with virtue and motherhood. These women can protest at the airport, as members have done on several occasions, without fear of violence—and knowing they will attract outsize media attention. They are also not a constituency that their senators want to cross.

"There is a privilege that we have not earned but that we have," Sharlee said. "No one is going to billy-club us, no one is going to hit us or gas us. We're Mormon women! We'll bring cookies!" She smiled. "So we have to claim that privilege and use it for the good of our vulnerable brothers and sisters. It is our responsibility to do that."

Three days after Sharlee received the call about Avelar-Flores, MWEG and the leaders of Salt Lake Indivisible called a rally outside the ICE offices. Addressing the crowd through a bull-horn, Sharlee said, "We will mourn with those who mourn, comfort those who need comfort, and bear the burdens of our fellow men and women." Two days later, Garn called Sharlee: if MWEG could make sure that Avelar-Flores's lawyer filed a form that day, Hatch would stay her deportation. Sharlee stood over the lawyer while he did it.

A few weeks later, Sharlee and I got in her car and drove to West Jordan for an activists' meeting about fighting uneth-ical deportation under the Trump administration. Represen-tatives from the ACLU, Utah Coalition of La Raza, Action Utah, Showing Up for Racial Justice, Holy Cross Ministries, and every other significant progressive lobbying organization in Utah were in attendance.

"We are newcomers to this," Sharlee told the group mod-estly, by way of introduction. "And we're here to learn from you." She briefly explained MWEG's mission, its initiatives, its leadership, and its methods. The room was silent for a moment.

A lawyer from the ACLU spoke finally. "You all are way more sophisticated than you give yourselves credit for." Sharlee and the women smiled graciously, and continued the meeting.

As the days passed and I continued to zip around the Utah desert interviewing MWEG members, I was moved by the earnestness of their faith in their power to change huge sys-tems. This was June 2017, and it seemed that all anyone who voted against Trump wanted to talk about was how fucked we were, how incredibly fucked, and how stupid the other side was and didn't they deserve to lose their health care, and there was nothing anyone could do wasn't this simply the end of America what a tragedy but also good riddance.

If this is the cultural stew you swim in, there's something stunning about seeing a group of Americans who are not yet jaded about the limit of their power as citizens, who do not yet feel there's absolutely nothing they can do to change their country, because in some sense they're only just discovering they have meaningful civic power at all. Coming up against this energy for real, the down-to-the-toes belief in the citizen's ability to make big change in the culture of their nation, the faith of the underdog, was sort of a shock. Their idealism put me to shame.

When I was twenty-one and still an actor, I spent a year rehearsing and playing the role of Harper in *Angels in America*, a young Mormon woman who's lost the thread. She's a "jack" Mormon, she explains. "It means I'm flawed. Inferior Mormon product." Harper is disappointed by her faith, living in New York, and overly interested in what she sees when she takes Valium. It's suggested she's recently had a miscarriage. Her husband, Joe, is gay and trying not to be, and she loves him desperately, so she's going quietly and deliberately out of her mind.

Harper is a daughter of a religion that was born and nursed entirely in America, shot through with manifest destiny and westward expansion, defined by transnational migration, away from religious persecution and toward a Zion they found in the scalded deserts of Utah. Harper moves in the wrong direction and leaves Utah, reversing her ancestors' migration, following her husband.

I loved Harper. Everything is wrong with her, she's the exact opposite of what a Mormon woman is supposed to be, and yet she's engaged with some essential aspect of the story of Mormon women: vision, grit, survival. She is hurting and she is failing and she is extremely high most of the time, and still somehow she sees more clearly than anyone else. She's the play's most prophetic character—precisely because she doesn't have any idea how to cope with her own life, she apprehends the people around her and the cause and effect of the world better than anyone else. "I see more than I want to see," she confesses, sounding a little like Cassandra.

I think it was in the middle of rehearsing Harper that a friend showed me *Love Taza* for the first time. (Back then, the blog was called *Rockstar Diaries*.) Look at this woman and her adorable baby, my friend said. (Back then, there was only one baby.) This woman was the archetypal Mormon woman, the woman Harper was rather spectacularly failing to be. She looked so happy.

At the time I was perplexed about what life I might want, and in love with a man I thought I would probably marry. Even though something about that idea felt wrong to me, I became fascinated with *Love Taza* as a representation of the future into which I might throw myself: husband, babies, trips to the park, the transmutation of motherhood into a beautiful performance that would fulfill and sustain me. I knew, even then, that I wasn't a Naomi Davis and didn't really want to be, but I watched her the way you watch the girl you knew in high school, the one who became the woman you almost became, the near-miss shadow self.

One of Harper's functions in the play is to show us the pain of a disappointed promise. She married the handsome and good man and tried to give him children, but he cannot love her and she cannot bear his children. The disappointed promise is, as Kushner reminds us, a very Mormon experience, and a very American one. When she hears the story of the Mormon migration west to Salt Lake City, Harper laughs bitterly. "They drag you on your knees through hell and when you get there the water of course is undrinkable. Salt. It's a Promised land, but what a disappointing promise."

Later, after her husband has left her, when she is living more in Valium hallucinations than in reality, Harper dreams that a Mormon pioneer mother comes to her, straight-backed and weathered from her journey. "Bitter lady of the Plains, speak to me," Harper begs. "Tell me what to do." When the Mormon mother tells Harper to "ask something real," Harper thinks for a moment, and then poses the central moral question of the play. "In your experience of the world, how do people change?"

How do people change?

When the boyfriend and I finally parted ways, I returned to this moment in the play, as I have periodically since then, every time the situation feels impossible, every time I feel lost, or wrong, or jack. The power of the Mormon woman, as Kushner wrote her—or of anyone who is set on a fixed and inexorable path of who and how to be—is that if she chooses to leave her path, she knows more than you ever will about how to make a new world.

After a beat, the Mormon mother tells Harper that when people change it's because they were forced. God splits their skin and reaches in them and grabs their insides hard and pulls and "they slip to evade his grasp but he squeezes hard, he insists, he pulls and pulls till all your innards are yanked out." Then he puts them back, rearranged and torn. "It's up to you to do the stitching," she says.

Joe comes back to Harper, but eventually she leaves him. The last time we see her, it's on a night flight to San Francisco, which, in the world of the play, looks a lot like heaven.

PHONE CALLS FROM
THE APOCALYPSE

Nearly every day now my phone rings from a number unknown to me. The area codes are always Californian, and always new. The calls started from cities in or near Los Angeles: Culver City, Inglewood, Marina del Rey. Then, once I stopped picking them up, they'd come from farther north: Merced, Turlock, Patterson, Stockton.

My parents still live in California, so when I saw unlisted California numbers, I'd think that one of them was in the hospital and I was being notified. I'd pick up, worried, and hear a long silence. Then a man's voice would say: "First they deceived you, then they oppressed you."

The voice is clearly a recording—there's something scratchy about the line, some ambience behind him that sounds canned. His diction is familiar to me from memories of old televangelists and Pentecostal preachers, though I can't tell from his voice where in the country he might be calling from. The way he speaks is stylized; every consonant is rhythm, every word is beaten through the teeth. He sounds like he's trying to exorcise you over the phone.

"There is a person keeping you in this situation," he says, every time. "Press the numerical button one, press one now." From there it deviates, but it's variations on a theme. Here's what he said on October 2: "There is someone you must rebuke that is attacking you. Press the numerical button one now, press one now. There is an individual causing this situation that you must rebuke, press one, press one. You must rebuke the snake that is controlling the person to cause this mess, press one. It has even been affecting people in your household. Press one now, press one."

The first time I got the call, I was so stunned by its vehemence that I didn't hang up. I sat there, clutching my cell phone to my ear all the way through the man's exhortations to press the numerical button 1 until the line seemed to go dead. Then, another man's voice came on the line, a different man, who was speaking normally, like any regular telemarketer. "If you'd like to continue, press one now. If you'd like to no longer receive these calls, press four."

I hesitated. The obvious thing to do would be to press 4, but I was curious. I badly wanted to see what would happen if I pressed 1, but that way lay the robocall deluge. Instead, I did nothing and waited. Eventually, the call disconnected.

Since that afternoon, now almost a year ago, I receive these calls most days. Sometimes I pick up, sometimes I don't. They started to become part of the cadence of my week, a visitation from some other corner of the country, though I'm never sure

where. Sometimes my phone will ring in the middle of dinner with friends and I'll check it, only to put the phone back
down when I see the unfamiliar California number. "It's just
the apocalyptic preacher calling."

The scripts of the calls aren't always precisely apocalyptic,
but they are formulated as a warning. I got a call from Oakland
as I was walking up Sixth Avenue in the West Village. "Hello?"

"I saw the spirit of witchcraft, someone was trying to ma-
nipulate you. Press the numerical button one."

Visiting my brother in Los Angeles, I got a call from
Fresno. "There is someone who has your name in their mouth.
Press the numerical button one. You have always been uneasy
about them and this is why, press one. You used to be around
them and things are coming up now. Ushebe—press one, press
one. We must break this thing before sundown, please press
the numerical button one now."

Your situation is bad, the caller wants to convince you. You
sensed it, and you were right. Someone is trying to cause you
harm, and they're succeeding.

It's all very strange, but there are years when it might
have seemed stranger. The news is only vaguely less eschato-
logical. The Ku Klux Klan is marching with torches through
the streets of Charlottesville. Children are being held in cages
at the border. Mass shootings roll in weekly at schools, syna-
gogues, concerts: eleven dead, fifty-nine dead, seventeen dead.
The deceased owner of a brothel called the Moonlite Bunny
Ranch was posthumously elected to the Nevada state legisla-
ture. Five million acres burned; "historic" floods; "once in a
generation" storms. So many people die of opioid overdoses

that the national life expectancy falls for the first time in fifty years. North Korea brags that its missiles can easily reach Hawaii, and the United States dissolves its nuclear nonproliferation agreement with Russia. Climate scientists revise an earlier prediction that a two-degree rise in earth temperature would be irreversibly catastrophic to say that actually 1.5 degrees will do the trick, a point of no return for the planet that they're expecting to arrive not in fifty years but in fifteen.

In late 2018, poor Sam Sifton, a food critic, opened his normally cheery weekend column of recipe suggestions with the line "It just keeps getting worse, is what it seems like." The mood is generally dark.

In these days, when scientists are talking about an actual end to the world and things seem to be coming apart at the seams on basically every social and political front, the phone calls sound almost reassuringly in touch with the spirit of the times: this is going badly.

Even the language the evangelist uses in his pitch for "the numerical button one" sounds familiar. This was the call from Oakland on September 25: "They can no longer mess with your stuff. This has happened because of what they tried to mess with that is YOURS. Press the numerical button one now. God is about to go before you to fight what they're trying to do TO you, press the numerical button one now. These are individuals that the enemy is using and institutes that the enemy is using to come against you. Press one, press one."

And another, on October 13, from Calistoga: "They will not take anything else from you. They tried to take your family your money your joy your peace your happiness, press one press one, they will not be able to take anything else from you this is the end of it enough is enough. Press the numerical button one. You thought you would have been out of it by this year, you thought you would have been taken care of by now, press one press one."

This is the era of being "robbed," the year of the con artist, the time of everyone losing out to someone else. Immigrants are coming to take your jobs, Republicans are coming to take your health care, angry women are coming for men's reputations and careers, straight white men are coming for your bodily autonomy, the police are coming for your life, trans people are coming for your bathrooms, the Democrats are coming for your guns, Silicon Valley is coming for your privacy, left-wing snowflakes are coming for your free speech, oil companies are coming for your land, and on and on. It's an incomplete list—and naturally some of these fears strike me as well founded while others seem horrendously misplaced—but the rhetoric of persecution has become the national common denominator. The apocalyptic telephone preacher knows this. Someone is taking away from you what is rightfully yours, he says. There is someone to blame for your troubles and I know who it is.

I keep waiting for this man to ask me for money. It's curious that a call of this nature doesn't come right out with a request, something along the lines of "For only six hundred and sixty-six dollars you can know the name of this usurper and I'll smite him for you." I can only assume that if I were ever to go ahead and press the numerical button 1, I'd be transferred to some kind of donation hotline or my number would be sold to hundreds of other evangelists, since, further research shows, robo-evangelism is its own cottage industry. But he never comes right out and asks. Instead he says simply, I know what ails you. You can know, too.

Lately, it doesn't seem like what ails any one of us is simple enough for that. It's a big, ailing world, and like an idiot I keep picking up the phone. Not every day, but enough that it's irrational. I keep wondering what he'll say.

SHAKERS

Imagine them in their straight rows: straight backs, straight bonnets. In the morning they wake up in their straight and narrow beds, unhang the clothes they hung on the pegs fastened carefully into their plain bedroom walls, clothes with even and straight seams, clean run-stitches. They walk down twin staircases, out onto twin porches, through twin doors into the hall of worship, which is just a plain room with two even rows of straight wooden benches.

In there, they whirl and whirl.

Imagine them always facing each other, the men and the women, looking across the twin banisters of their clean and simple houses, and never touching. To become a Shaker you had to join the community of your own free will, signing over all your property to the group, dissolving any marriage or family unit that might have held you before. Children were parted from their parents and sent to live in the children's house, supervised by a few elders, and husbands and wives would part to live in the same house built in a mirror image of itself: the men's quarters on one side, the women's on the other. It was forbidden to pass between them.

There was only one Family, with God at its head, and people were only ever Brothers and Sisters. The community discouraged any kind of special friendship, even platonic, because that way lay attachment, ownership, greed, factionalism, mine-ness and yours-ness. There was only the great Ours. Up in Heaven, God was also divided down the middle, a Father God and a Mother God.

Their spaces were designed to permit almost no privacy. The Shaker pegs that eventually became famous in American home design were created so that everyone's belongings stayed visible. Brethren slept in communal rooms with twin beds, and they were regularly rotated from bedroom to bedroom so that they wouldn't get too attached to any one space or any one roommate. The mechanism of their intimacy was mostly their eyes: if they couldn't touch each other or even prefer each other, they could look at each other.

When, in 1821, the Shakers codified their laws for the first time, a peculiar number of them had to do with interior design:

> Bedsteads should be painted green. Blankets for outside spreads should be blue and white but not checked or striped; one rocking chair in a room is sufficient except where the aged reside. One table, one or two stands, a lamp stand may be attached to the woodwork if so

desired. One good looking glass, which ought not to exceed eighteen inches in length and twelve in width, with a plain frame. No maps, charts, and no pictures or paintings shall ever be hung up in your dwelling rooms, shops, or Office.

Other religions have odd, fussy rules for the banal details of daily life, but the Shakers' were especially visual. They believed that the perfection of God could and should be mirrored by perfection of the material world they built around themselves. The beauty of their design is a strange beauty. They believed in square forms and straight lines. Walls always meet at right angles and have square or rectangular lines; paths, too, are laid at right angles, with no diagonal shortcuts. Curves appear only when necessary to improve the function of a design, say in a banister or a round barn, because Shakers refused to manifest anything into the world that was ornamental. Everything existed to be useful, even people. "Hands to work, hearts to God" was the guiding principle of the community, and work was their great spiritual practice, inseparable from worship. Their spaces were clean and undistracting, spiritually and literally. Once a year, they went through their buildings and ritually swept out all the ungodliness.

The shapes this ideology produced, and the feeling it gave the people who entered their spaces, were strange and compelling. Thomas Merton wrote that "the peculiar grace of a Shaker chair is due to the fact that it was made by someone capable of believing that an angel might come and sit on it." Laymen may not have understood why they liked the Shaker chair, but they liked it sufficiently that the chairs began to sell and then Shaker pegs began to sell; their round stone barns began to replicate across the countryside, their flat brooms appeared in kitchens, their window sash counterweights, their rotary saws, their clothespins, their staircases, their rocking chairs, their storage chests. The country and then the world grew saturated by their way of seeing interior spaces, while they stayed in their workshops and their mirror-image houses, quietly and diligently working.

All this was contrasted by a quirk of their worship: it was ecstatic, cathartic. At first they simply shook and shook, overcome, which is how they got their name, "The Shaking Quakers." Initially, the shaking was simply a way of letting go of lust or other troubling energy, or expressing joy. Later, they danced, ritually, during their meetings, precise and coordinated dances: the Round, the Hollow Square, and the Square Step; the Circular and Square and Compound Marches. They practiced these dances so they could be done without partners, and without anyone calling the steps. They also called this dancing "laboring."

It's about the most compelling thing I've ever heard, a group of radical ascetics living in their own corners of forest all the way from Maine to Kentucky, forsaking all desire, all intimacy, all possessions, all wanderlust—to carve perfectly designed wooden pegs and dance perfectly geometrical dances. Who among us hasn't had the fantasy of escaping into some system of blinding simplicity and idealism so engrossing that it, all by itself, is enough for you for the rest of your life?

For a long time the Shakers were able to sustain themselves based on the beauty and radicalism of their oddness. They were ahead of nearly every social justice movement in U.S. history. Before slavery was abolished, the Shakers were accepting black Americans as equal brothers and sisters. Decades before women had the right to vote, they were equal partners in the leadership of the Shaker church, where the prophet was a woman: Mother Ann Lee. The Shakers taught all children to read, so orphans were routinely dropped at their doors, and poor people sent their children to be raised and schooled at the colonies.

At the height of the church, there were about six thousand brethren in America, spread across nineteen settlements. Now there are two: Brother Arnold Hadd and Sister June Carpenter, who live together at the last active Shaker colony, in Sabbathday Lake, Maine. Until 2017, there was a third, Sister Frances Carr. It was not a way of life that perpetuated itself naturally, partly because it permitted no progeny but also because asking people not to love, not to attach, requires something most people can't manage. Is that why the ones who did made such spectacular furniture? Their influence is everywhere, sitting in our houses, lurking in a recurring faddish desire for clean lines and minimalism. Every time the world gets to be too much, American interior design skitters back toward a Shaker ethic: away from ornament and complication, away from French provincial or Art Deco, back toward ethereal simplicity. You likely have sat in a Shaker chair, or a knockoff of one, without realizing an angel was meant to sit there.

I drove up one winter Sunday to see the Shaker colony at Sabbathday Lake. I wanted, in the tradition of the Shakers, to see it with my own eyes, to take them in visually. I had seen so many photos of their interiors—long, high-ceilinged meeting halls with curved arches in the twin doors for men and women to enter; hand-hewn dormers lighting attics lined with built-in dressers for storing winter clothes; the elegant taper of staircase banister spindles; adult-sized rocking cradles designed to soothe the sick and elderly. It made me feel calm, looking at their interiors.

While that region of Maine is exquisite, it's dreary in February, and the Sabbathday Lake colony wasn't particularly visually appealing from outside. It's just off a strip of highway, a few hundred yards of dirt road linking simple white clapboard buildings standing at right angles to one another, and behind that, a farm. Several dozen sheep stood in the cold, their wool long and matted.

Inside, however, the dwelling house was large and beautiful and simple, with pegs on the walls and Shaker chairs, everything as you might expect it. I made my way to the meeting room and entered through the women's door. Immediately, I was hailed by Sister Frances Carr, the last woman alive to have been raised a Shaker from childhood. She was dressed in a long, high-necked purple dress in the traditional style. "Do you want to sit over there," she asked, pointing at one empty bench, "or over here? Here," she said, "come sit right here." She beckoned me to the front row, beaming. The benches were sparsely populated by visitors, neighbors, and official Friends of the Shakers—people who are involved in the colony but are not fully committed themselves.

The Sunday meeting was structured similarly to a Quaker meeting, where you stand and speak if you have something to say, and where long silences pass. In those silences, we sat, over on the women's side, and looked across at the men, who sat on their own benches opposite, looking at us. The benches were not uncomfortable, but neither were they comfortable.

It was a moment of temporal flattening in the way old rituals often are, when you can feel yourself echoing the gestures of people long dead. We were dressed differently from how the brethren used to be, and of the fifteen or so people in the room, only three were actually brethren. But it was the same room, and it was Sunday, and people stood and spoke, and others stood and replied in song. We sat and looked at one another more.

I spent much of that time wondering about whether it's possible to create something perfect, something that completely expresses the hope for living in radical freedom and radical equality and radical spiritual enlightenment, without sublimating all other desire into the effort. You have to imagine that there might not have been quite the emphasis on (or time for) perfect stitches and perfect methods had they been permitted particular love, or sex, or anything that existed purely for nonfunctional pleasure. It may be that the moment for that kind of self-abnegating attention to detail as an organizing principle for an entire society has passed, or is passing. The writer Mary Ruefle, upon visiting a Shaker colony, was most compelled by their graveyard. "Standing there one is confronted with the real Shaker theme—a simple, empty meadow full of the dead who have been stripped of their names like the anonymous burying grounds of war, all individuals gone to a greater cause."

After the service I stayed for a doughnut, but left fairly quickly. I needed to get back on the road. Leaving town, I stopped at a gas station to fill up my tank. As I set the nozzle in the filler neck, I realized that there had been something missing from the service, something that I suppose is already entirely extinct. I clicked the clip into the handle so the nozzle would stay in place and I could have my hands free. According to my own awkward rhythms, in full view of all the down-easters filtering in and out of the station shop for coffee and cigarettes, I danced a little dance. It was less a dance than a wiggle, an homage but also a mini-catharsis of the fine posture and right angles of the morning. The original dances weren't improvised like this. The dancers trembled fiercely, but within their smooth-planed walls. They walked deliberately and ceremonially in concentric circles, coming back always to where they had been, as they knew they would.

A THEORY OF
IMMORTALITY

There's a section of the Fishlake National Forest in Utah where the quaking aspens seem to take a little more space for themselves. The ground between white trunks lengthens and the sunlight gains more traction on the leaves, which are the color of jade in the summer and amber in the fall. The leaves tremble furiously even in a slight breeze.

This corner of forest—thousands of trees, roughly thirteen million pounds of biomass—is actually one living organism, a single rhizome that's been replicating and replicating, sending up new tree shoots as others die, for millennia. The exact age is unknown, but it's estimated to be between eighty thousand and a million years. This means that, conservatively, this organism has been alive since humans began to use tools, and possibly since we discovered fire. In this time, it has grown to be the largest known living organism, and for its Methuselaic achievements it has earned itself a name: Pando. Pando is beautiful, male, gigantic, theoretically immortal, and possibly dying.

What does it mean to be theoretically immortal? Michael Grant, one of the scientists who brought Pando to public attention, explained that quaking aspens reproduce both sexually, through seeds and flowers, and asexually, in clones, by sending new root suckers out underground. (This dual method of reproduction is an important factor in clonal aspens' remarkable ubiquity; it is the most widely distributed tree in North America.) Because of this manner of reproduction, Pando could just keep going forever. "There's a lot of biology that doesn't age and die," Grant wrote to me, but we don't always know why. He cites Henrietta Lacks as an example: the cervical cells taken from her body in 1951 have reproduced an entire generation each day ever since. Human cells, as a rule, die eventually, and they tend to die fairly rapidly in culture. Though Lacks died shortly after the sample was taken, her cells did not. They are, for reasons unknown, apparently immortal human cells.

But while Lacks's cells continue to reproduce wildly in laboratories all over the world—scientists estimate that if you piled all the Lacks cells ever grown on a scale, they'd weigh more than fifty million metric tons and wrap around the earth three times—Henrietta Lacks herself, as known to her children and friends, is long dead. The persistence of her biological material, now far older and greater in scale than she ever was, has raised questions about whether they constitute something resembling human immortality: Does the persistence of Lacks's cells grant her a kind of afterlife, albeit biological rather than spiritual? Where, in the millions of tons of Lacks, is Henrietta?

Pando and other clones like it—there are many thousands in North America, possibly some even larger than Pando—inspire similar inquiries. Pando's individual trees are born, age, and die, but the clone itself, the organism united by a single genetic code and a massive underground root structure, persists. When some of its trees are killed off by fire or storm, energy transfers through the roots and stimulates new growth elsewhere. Karen Mock, the geneticist currently heading up research on Pando, suspects that none of the tissue from the first tree remains. "The intangible is more persistent than the individual embodiments of it over time," she wrote to me. Pando is large enough to be resistant to total wipeout by a single natural disaster, so its cyclic growth could carry on infinitely.

I once had a disagreement with a boyfriend about the details of this process. The dispute was more semantic than factual. He described organisms like Pando this way: aspen trees "share their roots"; they reach out underground and clasp onto one another as if holding hands. They survive collaboratively. I insisted that the trees weren't holding hands. They were the same tree at root, shooting up many varied expressions of itself, a triumphant single organism. He saw a collective and I saw an individual—which, he observed pointedly, seemed like a pretty decent metaphor for some more critical differences in our dispositions. I rolled my eyes.

Organisms like Pando resist metaphors like the ones we were somewhat clumsily trying to assign them. They demonstrate that distinctions like individual versus collective are contingent on our own narrow perceptions of time and scale. They also suggest that our most common assumptions about individuality are limited and perhaps limiting. Like Pando, the human body regenerates and replaces itself over time. Our bodies experience total cellular turnover roughly every seven years, which means that the cells that constituted us at birth are gone and gone and gone again—but we are still here. Still, hiking through Pando, one sees many trees, clustered together but distinct, just as when walking through a crowded city avenue you see the swarm but feel even more intensely your own singular movement through it, your individual body as alike but separate from other bodies.

"Our bodies prime our metaphors, and our metaphors prime how we think and act," writes the journalist James Geary. Eula Biss, who quotes Geary early in her book *On Immunity*, points out that the perception that we are physically discrete, distinct, closed systems protected by a boundary of skin, infects our metaphors as much as it informs our social and medical decisions. This perception is inherently flawed. Bodies are open systems, and their survival doesn't rest simply on the individual immune system but on herd immunity, the reliance of our health on the health of those around us. "Our bodies may belong to us, but we ourselves belong to a greater body composed of many bodies," Biss writes. "We are, bodily, both independent and dependent." In another moment, Biss cites the science writer Carl Zimmer, who happens to be speaking of humans and viruses but could just as well be summarizing Biss's general philosophy: "There is no us and them."

There's been a flurry of concern about Pando in the last few years because, though it is immortal in theory, the clone appears to be in danger of dying. The possible reasons for this are many and imperfectly understood. There have been severe droughts, real estate development, and a surge of insects. Animals have overgrazed the tender young tree shoots, killing off new growth. Fire prevention efforts have, counterintuitively, deprived the tree of the periodic burns crucial to its life cycle. In this respect, Pando is one high-profile victim of sudden aspen decline, the mass die-off of thousands of quaking aspens all over North America that scientists have been tracking since roughly 2004. Pando's survival depends on its ability to regenerate, and after many millennia this is proving harder than it used to be. Its older trees remain, but the young ones aren't flourishing as they should, which means that the average age of trees in the stand is rising precipitously. The clone is facing a struggle we recognize: it is aging.

In Utah, Karen Mock's team is fencing off Pando's new growth to protect it from grazers, and working quickly to understand the sudden decline. If drought and rising temperatures are the true culprit, there may be little they can do. It would be unsettling to watch Pando die. The death would have the flavor of extinction—not just because sudden aspen decline raises the threat of extinction for North America's most ubiquitous tree, but because the death of this single clone will also be, as my ex would point out, the death of many interconnected individuals. As is typical for quaking aspens, every tree in the clone is an exact copy of the one next to it—the same leaf patterns, the same black scarring on the trunks. In a small corner of Utah, it has been possible, nearly forever, to get lost in miles of this one particular pattern making itself again and again.

Here I'm dangerously close to straying into sentiment, which was what so irritated me about that ex-boyfriend's insistence on the aspens' holding hands. For some reason it's difficult to be impassive about trees, difficult to see them clearly. Since the Tree of Life, a mytheme common to ancient religions from every corner of the world, we have been telling stories about trees to tell stories about ourselves, and so it's hard to resist our desire to make the tree a story, to make it our story, to make it us. We've turned them into oracles, goddesses, ancestors, external souls, sympathetic witnesses of our sorrow, absorbers of our illness, living temples, axes mundi that hold up the cosmos and connect heaven and earth.

Pando is older than all this, too—older even than our oldest stories. It is also only one clone of millions. They have been shivering and dying for so long. We continue with our Sturm und Drang, playing with fire and holding hands with ourselves.

THE OTHER CITY

Say you are found on your bathroom floor, on the grassy knoll of someone else's front yard, in the berth of your tractor trailer, in your own bed, at the foot of a bridge, under a car wheel, in the car, caught in the bend of a river, collapsed in the bar, alone in the remains of a scorched kitchen. Your death is sudden and unexpected, a death no one plans for but that approximately half a million of us will experience this year in America. No death is special, but this kind of death requires special care, procedurally, from a number of people you will never meet. The procedural aspects of your death, which you will never see, begin with a phone call.

One afternoon in the summer of 2018 in Cleveland, a man came home to find his wife slumped over her computer keyboard. She was in her fifties and had been in poor health, but nothing had seemed urgent or life-threatening. It looked like she'd died while shopping online. Her husband called 911.

When officers from the Cleveland Police Department arrived at the house and viewed the scene, they weren't entirely sure what had happened. It looked like maybe a cardiac episode, or a seizure, or an overdose. The woman had a long list of prescription medications, and in Ohio, one epicenter of the opioid crisis, most untimely deaths with no obvious foul play are marked for further investigation. The officers called the medical examiner's office. A death investigator named Erin Worrell picked up.

As a death investigator for the Cuyahoga County medical examiner's office, Worrell serves as "the eyes, ears, and nose" of the forensic pathologists who perform autopsies, determine cause and manner of death for the public record, and sign death certificates. It's often said that death investigators are "the last of the first responders," in that their task begins when the initiatory drama of the death scene ends. Worrell's job is to collect the man who jumped in front of the train, learn what type of train it was, how fast it was going, and how its brake system works; to search for drugs so they can be tested; to count gunshot wounds and identify corresponding bullets in the walls. Worrell is forty but looks much younger. She has infectious enthusiasm and the gruff, game pragmatism sometimes found in women who work in physical, male-dominated fields. She loves her job.

When she got to the scene, roughly thirty minutes after the officers called, the woman's neighbors and family had heard the news and were starting to appear, shaken, at the front door. Worrell began the standard investigation for a scene of this sort, asking the husband when he last talked to his wife, when he came home, what her medical history was, whether he had any concerns or suspicions about her cause of death. She inspected the woman's body to see whether her lividity patterns—which indicate the position of the body at the time of death—matched the husband's story. She talked to the police officer to check her information against his, and inspected the house for anything telling, like drug paraphernalia, weapons, or an open gas valve on the stove. She took photographs all the while and made copious notes for the woman's case file. Worrell confirmed what the detective had suspected: because there was no clear natural cause of death, the woman would need an examination and probably an autopsy.

There's an authority with which the mechanism of death investigation proceeds, one signaled by badges, checklists, jargon, a wealth of protocols. It leads swiftly and invariably to a moment of transition—the person on the floor becomes a body that no longer belongs to the people who know it, and the time comes to take that body away. Worrell took the husband aside and asked him to step out because they had to put his wife in a body bag, which he didn't need to see. He looked startled. This is a moment I have seen with other families—a hesitation to disassemble the death scene, however awful—the desire to create a catch step between the catastrophe and the silence that comes after. "Can we pray?" he asked finally.

"Sure," Worrell said immediately. "We can pray. I'll get anyone you want to come and pray." She called in the detectives and the contractors who were there to pick up the body and transport it to the medical facility, and asked them to stop what they were doing. She set down her clipboard and camera. The neighbors and friends who'd been arriving also came and all held hands. They said the Lord's Prayer.

Afterward, Worrell and the contractors resumed the routine: they lifted the woman into a body bag, zipped it shut, and loaded her into the van, which made its way to the innocuous office park in University Heights where the office of the Cuyahoga County medical examiner sits. The van went around back, to the wide bay door that serves as the entrance for what people working there call their "silent clients." Through that door is the morgue.

When you are born, you become what Dr. Glenn Wagner, medical examiner of San Diego County, calls "a legal person." Your whole life, until someone signs your death certificate, you remain a legal person with state and federal rights and, ideally, recourse if they get violated. "But when you die," Dr. Wagner explained over the telephone, "you stop being a legal person. You're now property that's handled, just like the dog, the cat, the bank account, or the house." You're subject to a hierarchy of inheritance, just like any other property, and the question of who owns your body depends on how you died.

There are five kinds of death, legally: accident, homicide, suicide, natural, and undetermined. If your death is categorized as natural—old age, known disease, anything expected and unpreventable—you belong to your family or next of kin. But if you die unnaturally—accident, homicide, suicide; or in circumstances of special interest to the state, like in a natural disaster or under legal custody—you become, even if just briefly, the property of the state. You are remanded into the care of your local coroner or medical examiner, whose job it is to determine which category your death belongs to as well as the specific manner of death, and then report that information to law enforcement and federal agencies, like the CDC or the DEA. Once they've done this, they sign your death certificate and return you.

"The kicker is," Dr. Wagner explained, "you're not dead until someone says you're dead." The mechanism of that declaration is the death certificate, which means that up until the moment the medical examiner signs your death certificate, you're not dead, legally. Nor are you technically alive. Each of us, no matter how we meet our ends, will someday enter this liminal state: legally property and so no longer a person; dead and legally alive.

The people who own you in this moment between physical death and legal death are medical examiners or coroners, depending on where you live. Medical examiners, in general, are forensic pathologists who have medical school training, plus a pathology residency, and then further training in forensics. Often, coroners are nonphysicians who work full-time in other professions, and in many places, like the state of Pennsylvania, the only requirements are to be eighteen, have lived in the county for one year, and have no felony convictions. Crucially, only a forensic pathologist can perform an autopsy. Ten years ago, the Justice Department issued a warning that there were fewer than five hundred forensic pathologists in the United States (for scale, there are nearly ten thousand dermatologists), a number that couldn't even half cover the rate at which we die in ways that require autopsy. In the years since, the opioid epidemic has increased their caseload so drastically that the system is on the verge of collapse. The last ten years have seen cascading office closures: forensic pathologists overburdened with too many cases lose accreditation with the national supervising association, and the bodies in their districts are shipped to other offices, which then get overloaded and risk losing accreditation in turn.

There are coverage deserts, huge swaths of—mostly rural—America left without easy access to autopsies or trained death investigators. For several months in 2015, anyone who died in Montana had to be transported to South Dakota if they needed an autopsy; in Wyoming, bodies often have to cross state lines because there are no forensic pathologists nearby. Oklahoma's overloaded medical examiner now declines to autopsy people over the age of forty who die of unexplained causes, as well as anyone who appears to have died by suicide. Chief medical examiners of Kentucky, New Jersey, New Hampshire, Los Angeles, and Cook County, Illinois (all offices serving millions of people), have resigned in protest over being asked to do too much with too little.

In 2016, news outlets reported that in Ohio bodies were being stacked two to a gurney and piled in refrigerator trailers rented to catch the morgue overflow. When *The Wall Street Journal* called the Cuyahoga County medical examiner Thomas Gilson for a quote, he compared it to a flood. "We're just really awash in drug deaths," he told the reporter. Cleveland has one of the largest and best-equipped facilities in the country, but it had a refrigerator trailer parked out back, too.

Before I arrived in Cleveland, I wasn't even sure what a medical examiner was or whether it was different from a coroner—which it is. But I had some impulse to witness the end of the body. If I could see that frightening truth, then—then what? Then I'd be prepared? Then I'd be able to more fully appreciate the body as a flawed but intact miracle when it is whole? I fear death, like anyone. Like anyone, I am occasionally struck into panic by the monumental reality that it is coming for me and everyone I love. I wanted to stand in the room with the body, after.

Foucault, writing about the graveyard as a heterotopia, supposed that Western culture became fixated on—and afraid of—the dead body in the same period of time that cemeteries were slowly evicted from the "sacred space" of the church, which sat at the heart of a city, and were moved to the outer borders of municipal spaces. People had once been buried in charnel houses or tombs where all bones were mixed together; now everyone had "his or her own little box for his or her own little personal decay." There arose, he writes, an "obsession with death as an 'illness'" that the living required protection against. He suggests this was related to a decentering of church life in general and the dissolution of the collective agreement concerning life after death.

"From the moment when people are no longer sure that they have a soul or that the body will regain life," Foucault writes, "it is perhaps necessary to give much more attention to the dead body, which is ultimately the only trace of our existence in the world and in language." If the end of the body is the end of the self, the corpse as an artifact becomes more precious, more individuated, and more frightening. The dead are banished to "the other city," where they can't infect our vitality.

People who work in medicolegal death investigation, as it's called, occupy one of the few remaining bridges between our city and the other, and their work remains almost entirely opaque to the people it serves—by the time laypeople experience it up close, they tend not to be in any position to report back.

I didn't know what meaning there might be in the end of the body, just as I don't know whether there's an end to the self, but I recalled Charon the Ferryman, the figure from Greek mythology who was charged with carrying souls across the rivers that divided the worlds of the living and the dead. Often he's portrayed as an old man or a gnarled half demon, standing in a boat holding a long oar. He's remote and fearsome by dint of his position, but still a kind of guardian—responsible for us as we undertake this brief, strange passage. The name "Charon," I learned, is derived from *charopós*, which means "of keen gaze." Charon, we are given to understand, is one who sees more than others.

On the plane to Cleveland I started making lists to steady myself:

Medical students see cadavers.
Morticians see cadavers.
Policemen and firefighters see them.
Nurses see cadavers.
Those clean-up crew people see cadavers.

I realized as I wrote that perhaps I should be more precise about the distinction to be made between a cadaver and a corpse.

Cadaver: from *cadere*, Latin, to fall. Tertullian was the first to use this particular euphemism: cadaver, the fallen one.

Not every body is a cadaver by virtue of being dead.

A cadaver is what we call a dead body when it's meant for dissection, a body that belongs to science.

When does a body turn into a corpse turn into a cadaver?

Another etymology for "cadaver," cited as folk etymology: from the Latin phrase *caro data vermibus*, "flesh given to worms."

"Corpse," by contrast, is a newer word, Middle English derived from Old French and originally, Latin: *corpus*, body. For centuries, "corpse," on the occasions when it was spelled with an "e," meant the body, the living body. Then, in the nineteenth century, the meanings split. "Corps" is the body—not just the living, breathing body, but the body politic, the body electric, esprit de corps. "Corpse" is the dead body.

Yesterday, a plane's engine exploded as it took off, breaking a window and nearly sucking a passenger out into the sky. The pilot, who had been among the first women to fly fighter jets for the air force, managed to land the plane safely, even with one engine and a hole in the fuselage. But the lady who was nearly sucked out the broken window went from corps to corpse. Now she's somewhere in a medical examiner's office in

Philadelphia, though she's from New Mexico, because your body belongs to the county where you died, not the place where you're from, which means that if this plane crashed, I'd belong to Ohio, which I've never seen.

Cleveland looks patchy green, gray, and ocher from above. It was April, and the pilot came over the loudspeaker to tell us it would be snowing on the ground. The landing was smooth.

"I learn something new every day here," Chris Harris said, escorting me into the warehouse full of mock death scenes. Harris is a smartly dressed man with a reassuring air of gentle competence about him. During the week, he runs communications for the medical examiner; nights and weekends he's a hip-hop artist.

The warehouse was glumly lit, and it smelled of earthy funk, which I suspected was decomposing evidence in the archives but turned out to be several pounds of marijuana that had been seized from a death scene. To our right, behind a wall of chain link, a dummy in a hoodie sprawled under a picnic table on bloody Astroturf, with a pistol near his rubber hand. Next door to him, a lady dummy in a housedress lay on the floor of a fake kitchen with the oven door open. The linoleum under her was dreary; her wig looked itchy.

The office of the Cuyahoga County medical examiner has the oldest forensic pathology training program in the country, and twice a year it hosts death investigation trainings for law enforcement, prosecutors, and coroners. These sets were constructed for their final test, where students assess each scene and make an initial determination. We walked through the array: a dummy sprawled in a giant pool of blood in a living room, a dummy collapsed in a faux jail cell, the suicide dummy under the park bench.

"You'll do this on Tuesday after you take the trainings," Harris said, guiding me through each room and grinning at my wrong guesses. The premise of these sets is that death can fool you if you don't know what you're looking at, and despite the garishness of the stiff-limbed dummies and the improbable redness of their blood, the point is made. I mistook a particularly gruesome-looking accident for a homicide, an overdose for a natural death, and I declined to venture a guess about what killed the dummy in custody, which was fine because Harris didn't remember how he died anyway.

When a dead person arrives at the morgue, they come around the back into a large garage, which has parking for a few cargo vans or hearses and two isolated bays where the city can tow cars for the investigators and pathologists to inspect. (Two days before I arrived, there was a drive-by shooting on a highway. The dead men were towed, still in their seats, and installed in the bay, where experts in trace evidence and ballistics drew thin hot-pink strings from the bullet holes in the windows to the holes in the bodies and seat cushions. By the time I saw it, their bodies had been lifted away and the bullets had been pried out from where they'd been buried. The car remained for the pathologists to examine, a standing artifact of violence. There was gluey brain matter on the cloth ceiling and blood in the cup holder.)

When bodies arrive, they are unloaded by a morgue technician and undressed. Clothes and jewelry go in a brown paper bag, which rests on the belly or at the ankles. Everything goes together onto a gurney, and then the body is weighed, finger-printed, photographed from all angles, and tagged with identi-fication numbers. The worst thing a medical examiner's office can do is lose you or swap you, and this isn't quite as rare as one would hope. In 2017, a family in California buried their son Frank, and eleven days later Frank came home. The guy they'd buried, whose name turned out to be John, was exhumed, cre-mated, and mailed back to Kansas.

Before they are bathed and restored by an undertaker, corpses look like clumsy imitations of human beings. They're too brittle, they're too still; their pallor is difficult to believe. Most of them were in bags, though occasionally an arm or a leg was visible, a bruise, pale toes. Only one head, and I looked at him last. His neck was rolled to one side, a double chin stiff as plaster.

Harris had warned me several times to prepare me for the smell, which is visceral and penetrating. The smell of death stays with you forever. When I was in the ninth grade, a rat died under a bank of lockers, and no one knew except that a funk seemed barely detectable in the air one day, and then a little stronger the next, until at the end of a week the smell was acrid, burning, radiating out of the room and down the hallway. I had never smelled a smell like that before—none of the thirteen-year-olds knew what it was. It smelled rounder than skunk, more salted than rotten fruit, deeper than latrines; it got into the back of your throat and stayed there. Oh, some grown-up said in instant recognition, something died.

I had worried before arriving in Cleveland that I might smell something I'd never be able to forget. It turned out, I already knew the smell. My nose recognized it the moment Harris ushered me into the refrigerator. Oh, I thought. Something died.

When we went into the isolated area where the office keeps bodies that are in states of advanced decomposition, the smell became impossible. A fingerprint expert dressed in scrubs and no mask was at work trying to retrieve a fingerprint off a man who was so far gone that his fingers had shrunk, hardened, and gone black. The expert cheerfully explained that there are a few ways to work this out. Sometimes boiling the finger works well because the tissue plumps back up briefly, long enough to get a print. Other times, and this is what he'd done today, you take advantage of something the skin of the hand will do all on its own during decomposition, something they call "degloving."

He slipped his hand inside the wet, delicate glove of the dead man's skin. It looked like the skin that forms over scalded milk, but transparent. He pushed his index finger all the way in to fill out every groove, and pressed it gently down on the inkpad.

"Are you okay?" asked Harris, dutiful shepherd. He meant, are you going to vomit, are you going to faint, are you going to cry.

"I'm fine," I told him. "It just smells horrible."

He laughed. "I don't even smell it anymore," he said. This seemed hard to believe.

The rest of the day, I felt like the smell had invaded my mucous membranes and lodged in the back of my throat. I recalled the scene in *Angels in America* when Louis says to Joe, "Do you know what smell is?"

"No," says Joe.

"We have five senses, and only two that go beyond the boundaries of ourselves . . . Know what a smell is?"

"It's . . . some sort of . . . no."

"It's made of the molecules of what you're smelling. Some part of you, where you meet the air, is airborne. Little molecules of Joe up my nose." In the play, this is a come-on, a suggestion that because these two men are standing close enough to smell each other, they're already engaged in a kind of mutual penetration. In the morgue, this sensory penetration is unsettling. For days and days, the smell of death clung to my clothes, my hair, my mouth.

At the Cleveland office, every morning begins with a staff meeting that includes all the forensic pathologists and at least one representative from every team that touches a body during its journey through their system: death investigators, morgue technicians, trace evidence techs, fingerprint specialists, toxicologists, drug chemists, and Harris. At 8:30 a.m., Dr. Gilson, the medical examiner, sweeps through the door to the conference room and shuts off the lights.

One by one, the cases that have come in since yesterday's meeting appear on the projector screen. The death scene photos taken by Worrell or one of the other investigators are clicked through in slideshow format while the deputy medical examiner, a thin, studious man named Dr. David Dolinak, reads aloud the case report. At this point, the coordination begins: if the case subject hasn't yet been identified, the fingerprints team and the death investigators will work with the identifications department to try to confirm an identity and next of kin. The pathologist doing the autopsy may request to inspect some items in the trace department, like a vial, spare clothing, or weapons recovered from the scene. Before the team moves on to another case, the initial determination is made: "We'll do an external examination," or "She is for autopsy."

The doctors never refer to their cases by name unless on the phone with a bereaved family member. If you are the 457th person to die in Cuyahoga County in the calendar year, you are Case 0457. Beyond that, they use only the description of your death. "The older lady whose husband found her at her desk" or "the thirteen-year-old who shot himself and there was suspicion of abuse" or "the guy they found in his trailer out on I-90." Your sex, your age, roughly, and the circumstances of your demise identify you to the people who know you in this phase of life.

On the day that I arrived, the workload was light. Everyone found it amusing that there was only one autopsy to recap. "Maybe you're a good omen," said one of the pathologists. "Maybe today we'll have one and tomorrow we'll have none!" They all laughed. "That'd be the day," someone chuckled.

Gilson invited me to chat after the meeting, and I followed him to his office, a wide-angled executive suite furnished with a giant wooden desk, a few microscopes, a tidy blue sofa, photographs of his mother, his mentor, and his children, and mountains of folders and loose-leaf papers. Gilson is a tall, generously proportioned man with a nearly inaudible speaking voice and floppy, curly hair. His wife had been begging him to get a haircut, but he maintains that he's fifty years old and he can grow his hair out if he wants. He was wearing a tie patterned in a Frank Lloyd Wright design because he was having his picture taken that afternoon. Later, the photographer would assure him that he didn't have to smile. "I like to smile," he protested mildly.

Gilson has a record of taking poorly functioning offices and restoring their accreditations and standard of care. He was brought to Cleveland in 2011 after a series of scandals led to a staff overhaul, and since then he's become a leading advocate for the role of forensic pathology in public health. He declined to tell me so himself, but the rest of his staff and various people at the Justice Department and the CDC let me know that he's been a major player in the public health response to the opioid crisis.

"I really feel like forensic medicine is kind of this undiscovered continent in public health," he explained, pushing his hair out of his face. "It has so many implications: gun violence, the drug crisis, natural diseases like the flu." Gilson often points out that the CDC statistics on injury and mortality are compiled from information drawn from offices like his, and that the level of investigation his team does on each case means they have a much richer source of data than can be communicated in CDC reports.

After realizing that in at least half their overdose cases there had been someone nearby who could have intervened well before EMS arrived, Gilson asked the city to provide Naloxone and training to the community. After noticing a trend of opiate overdose victims who were recently out of prison, the team created a program with local prison systems designed to educate inmates about the danger of fentanyl as part of their release. Gilson has a semiregular guest spot on local news to warn people about whatever's particularly dangerous at the moment—drownings in the summer, car accidents in the winter.

Later in the morning, I followed him up to the trace evidence department. He was scheduled to perform a demonstration autopsy for a group of young prosecutors, introducing them to the basics of death investigation. The decedent—their word for the deceased—for this demo was an elderly man who'd hanged himself, and Gilson wanted to inspect the rope.

"Whenever we have trace evidence, I have the option of coming down to take a look," he said. "We do it on all our homicide cases."

Gilson turned and began to handle the man's neck. He was laid out, naked and mottled, with the rope still attached and coiled near his head. Gilson glanced at Dan Mabel, a criminalist who works in the trace evidence department. "Do you have the gun for the other guy?"

Mabel shook his head, then explained to me that he was working on the case of a black teenager found with a gun in his hand and a gunshot wound to the head. Detectives had thought it was a homicide, but this team thought it was more likely a suicide.

"You know that's a rising trend, suicide among young African American males, that I haven't heard a lot about." Gilson lifted the rope off the older man's neck and turned it over in his hand, inspecting its weave and weight. "We tend to think about suicide as older white guys or middle-aged white guys. Which is still true, but if nobody's following trends . . ." He waved his hand toward the morgue.

The day before, another black teenager had arrived with a self-inflicted gunshot to the head. That morning, because most of the bodies in the fridge had been taken upstairs for autopsy already, he seemed alone in the cooling unit, laid out on a gurney in the very center as if on a pyre. When his age had been read aloud upstairs, a mournful breath had passed between the doctors. "Thirteen?" someone asked, as if hoping the number was wrong.

I asked him if this new problem seems to be local to Cleveland, and he shook his head. From what he was hearing by word of mouth, it was nationwide. Then again, he said, it's hard to know for sure. "I don't want to harp on this, but if you overburden the system with casework, the surveillance function is lost," Gilson said, finishing his check on the older gentleman and setting the rope back on the table. A critical part of their job is to keep an eye out for alarming trends, but when the medical examiners don't have time to collate their data and alert people to a pattern, like an epidemic of suicides among young black men, years can go by before anyone with the power to help even learns what's going on.

I noticed something on the wall behind Mabel's head: a cheery-looking poster with the suicide statistics for the year to date, emblazoned with the slogan SOARING TO NEW HEIGHTS AS OF MAY 14, 2018! Both men winced. "We keep track of the suicides," Mabel said, with a look of frustration and grief on his face. "We've just been slammed."

The autopsy techs are fond of saying that either you can handle an autopsy or you can't, and that there's no predicting whether you'll handle it until you personally see one and hit the floor, or don't. It is true that in the handful of autopsies I saw performed before a group, someone lost it. Curiously, no two people fell apart at the same moment, and some breaking points were puzzling. One young prosecutor remained hale as a rotary saw sliced off the top of a skull so the doctor could excavate the brain, but when the tech used a regular needle to draw blood from the big artery in the groin—rather demurely, I thought—she fainted.

Gilson in particular is charitable with guests about the fainting. "If you start to feel woozy or nauseous, it's totally okay," he says. "That's just your body telling you that what you're seeing is not natural." This explanation suggests that some part of your body will react to the sight of something unnatural happening to another body, regardless of what you intellectually know about the event you're witnessing. This is certainly what my body does, though I do not faint or vomit. Rather, I flush—adrenaline seizes me in certain parts of the procedure, during which I have to force myself not to bolt from the room. Unlike the woman who lost it at the sight of the needle, the parts I find most viscerally upsetting are the ones that most resemble desecrating a body or violating its privacy—cutting it open, sawing its bones, peeling the skin, scraping out its skull, slicing its organs, ruining it beyond repair. After the rotary saw, I was almost relieved to see the brain.

The inescapable and personally horrifying lesson of the autopsy is that there are moments in this process where it is not possible to treat the body gently. While it's clear that the physicians handle the body with immense care at every moment, there are many things they have to do that cannot be disguised as anything other than the total destruction of a body's wholeness. It is not violent in intention, but there's violence in the spectacle.

But not everyone feels this way. For a few days, I observed the work with a photographer named Sara Lewkowicz, and she remained more or less unmoved by the bloodier aspects of the autopsy she saw. She didn't even think they looked violent. "That's not a person anymore!" she said. "That's a shell." She got emotional about a dead woman's manicure. Whoever this woman was, we knew she was in her thirties and she died on her birthday. For a few days afterward, Sara kept bringing up the woman's fingernails. "She probably did her nails because it was her birthday and she was excited to go out and celebrate with her friends," she'd say, looking forlorn.

The doctor who did that autopsy is Liz Mooney. At thirty-five, she's the youngest forensic pathologist on staff, and she has lively eyes, a ready smile, and a certain obliging midwestern energy. Based on her general no-nonsense sunniness, I'd have guessed she was a second-grade teacher. After the autopsy, Mooney spent a few minutes making final notes and Sara and I stood around in the corner debating whether it would be possible to show in a magazine any realistic photos of what Mooney had just done. I was skeptical, suggesting that the visuals would be deemed too tough to handle. Sara agreed. "Too much gore," she said.

Hearing this, Mooney looked up from her clipboard. The autopsy tech, a man named Paul, was at work near the table in front of her, hosing blood and scraps of lung off the stainless steel table. He'd just finished peeling the woman's face back up off her neck and sewing it back over her skull. Mooney looked curiously at us, like we were missing the point.

"But some jobs are gory," she said kindly.

As I got further and further into this research, I became a nightmare at dinner parties. I strained to stay quiet in polite conversation. Now that I'd glimpsed this new world, I compulsively wanted to tell everyone. "Your dog will eat your face!" I wanted to yell. "It's more common than you think!" Little, white fluffy ones, Mooney told me, even ones with no record of aggression before or after. We don't know why. She's working on a paper about it.

Who wants to hear about these things over lasagna? "You can fracture nearly every bone in your body without breaking the skin! I saw it myself, a man who jumped off a bridge!" It's like a special kind of derangement. People kept catching me staring off into space, and when asked to explain myself I had to either lie or admit I was having a quick flashback to a teeny-tiny old lady who died falling down the stairs. When they opened her up they saw that her ribs had healed from more than thirty fractures over the years. It was sort of beautiful in the photograph, I want to tell them. I didn't know ribs could do that.

On my first trip to Cleveland, I went to a two-day forensics training that the Cuyahoga County medical examiner's office runs as part of its ongoing education efforts. The course is open to anyone to whom it might be professionally relevant, and people have come from as far as Nigeria to attend it, but the week that I joined the class the students were mostly local: a few forensic pathology fellows, criminal prosecutors and public defenders, emergency medical personnel, social workers, nurses, and several members of the Cleveland Police Department.

On the morning of the first day, we received a quiz. The questions ran in this general direction:

Fill in the blank: "A torn gunshot wound that can be put together again is _____."

TRUE or FALSE: While processing a hanging scene the ligature should always be removed from the decedent on scene.

All of the following are commonly seen in pedestrians who have been struck and killed by a motor vehicle EXCEPT: fractures of the lower legs, laceration of scalp, chop wound of buttocks, fractures of ribs.

The lessons proceeded, in one-hour increments, to offer all the knowledge you'd need to correctly answer a quiz of this kind. One by one, the pathologists took the podium at the front of the building's conference room. Liz Mooney taught us, with generous use of visual aids, how to identify the way bullets will stipple the skin while entering the body versus exiting, and how to recognize on sight the difference between a stab wound with a kitchen knife and one with a razor or piece of glass. Another doctor covered drownings; a third, car accidents; Erin Worrell explained how to identify an accidental infant suffocation, and demonstrated how she interviews grief-stricken parents using a life-size baby dummy. We learned to recognize how the body looks after poisonings, deaths in custody, hangings, bludgeonings, crushing, smothering, flaying, falls down flights of stairs, falls out of trees, hypothermia, hyperthermia, fire. We learned to recognize the characteristic forward slumping position of people who died of opioid overdoses, which is sometimes referred to as the prayer position. We learned to look at a corpse and its damage or rot as a story.

At the 2 p.m. break, I called my mother to recite all the things I now feared:

bees
house pets
lightning
propellers
putting cushions near infants
ice picks
icicles
fire
fire extinguishers

bodies of water
bathtubs
boats in general

"You're a delight right now," she replied. I reminded her to double-check the safety mechanism on her inversion table, because I heard a story about a man who got stuck upside down on one and asphyxiated.

At a point, the amount of power these people carry began to seem overwhelming. One afternoon, during the end-of-day meeting in Cleveland, the team began to discuss an autopsy Dr. Dolinak had performed that day on a baby from another county. For contract autopsies like this, the forensic pathologist can't make the decision about how to assign cause and manner of death—instead, they send their autopsy notes back to the local coroner, who can choose to certify the death in accordance with those findings or not. Dolinak's case was a difficult one, and perhaps because he's a veteran of the field and likes being collegial and useful to the younger pathologists, he offered it to the room as a test:

This infant was in the care of her father and grandfather, and they all went out to an event. Dad and Grandpa left her strapped into her car seat with the windows closed, and the weather was well into the nineties that day. The men said that they forgot about her for several hours, and when they realized their mistake and rushed back to the car, they found her dead. Do you rule this a homicide or an accident?

His question was a medical one, not a legal one: writing

"homicide" on a death certificate simply denotes "death at the hands of another person," and any non-accident meeting that description should be marked that way. The room was quiet for a moment. Most of the people in the room were themselves parents. "Homicide," suggested Liz Mooney. "You are responsible for the care of that person who can't take care of themselves. And you are responsible for that death. I would happily call it a homicide."

"I don't know," said Todd Barr, the office's newest pathology hire. "I think I would go accident. There was no mal intent."

Mooney interrupted him. "We don't use intent for homicide." Barr laughed a little at the abruptness of her interjection. "All right, I'll go undetermined then," he said. "I have a hard time pulling the H on this."

"I don't, actually," said Gilson. "It's unlikely he had intent, but this is a foreseeable outcome of somebody who was left in a hot car. Whether they intended to or they forgot . . ."

"Well, that's the part that really bugs me!" Barr made as if to smack his forehead. "It's like, how do you put an infant into a seat in the back of a car and say, Oh, I forgot! That does upset me."

Mooney shrugged. "I believe that people can forget. However crazy it is that people would forget. But that still doesn't make the fact that you're responsible for that infant—"

"Well, right," said Gilson. "I'm not saying murder, I'm saying homicide. Dolinak?"

"I'd probably go accident."

Gilson's eyebrows shot up. "Would you really!"

Dolinak shrugged. "That's what I've called cases like this

in the past. I use the same analogy, leaving a kid in the bathtub and it drowning. I would usually call those an accident unless there's something egregious or super negligent going on."

"But they always did something negligent," Gilson protested. "If they genuinely didn't intend for that outcome, it's for the legal system to try them and decide."

Barr interjected to bring up another case, one of a boy who couldn't use his arms and legs, and drowned in the bathtub. His mother had left for several days and put him in the care of a younger sister. One night the girl was bathing her brother and went into the other room for a few minutes to do something, which she thought was okay to do because the tub didn't have a drain stopper. Something—a washrag, maybe—got stuck in the drain, and when she came back he had drowned.

"We talked through that one a lot," said Barr, "and I think we came down on accident for that because . . . my gosh. This poor girl."

"Yeah, so that's an interesting scenario," said Dolinak, "because if you call it homicide, it's homicide by the sibling through the mom . . . or by the mom through the sibling?"

At this point, I interrupted to pose a question. My habit had been to sit in the back of these meetings silently, but seeing them stumbling through this totally normal, human, moral back-and-forth was perturbing. "Your feelings of compassion for the person who would be ruled to have committed homicide," I asked, "to what extent is that supposed to factor into a medical decision?"

"Not at all," said Mooney.

"But homicide under our jurisdiction is a medical diagnosis," Barr said.

"Right," I said. "So why would it then make a difference how bad you feel for the girl?"

Barr sat back and sighed. "It's a good point."

"Doesn't it influence the case an attorney can then make for charges?" Mooney asked. "I think us ruling it a homicide can then play a part in how they choose to charge an individual."

This went on for a while, until finally the group arrived at a stalemate. Gilson turned to Dolinak. "Know what you're gonna rule?"

Dolinak laughed. "Nope. That was a good discussion, though. Thanks, everybody."

The next day, I stopped by Dolinak's office to see what he'd decided. It seemed irreconcilable to me, even surreal, that the power to effectively create the most significant medical fact of this baby's life—did she die by accident or at the hands of her father—rested with him. That there's just some guy who makes those decisions, and that in this case he was the guy.

Dolinak cheerfully reminded me that that discussion had just been pretend, for practice. That infant was a contract case from another county, so her death was someone else's decision.

One might reasonably assume that there might be something strange about people who work in death investigation or perform autopsies. Certainly it is unusual to eagerly volunteer to analyze a body that's been sheared in half by a train, or to collect death paraphernalia in your office, or to amass a decades-long collection of forensically noteworthy death scene images—examples I am not inventing. But as a group, the pathologists, coroners, and autopsy techs I met were affable and regular, with families and hobbies so normal it all verged on bland. There were common quirks: Nearly all of them mentioned a love of puzzles like Rubik's Cubes or jigsaws. Many were fond of mysteries and thrillers. They all had steely stomachs and deep stoicism in the face of sights and smells that regularly make outsiders faint or vomit. Many mentioned feeling a fond and protective alienation from people in their lives who walked around without the constant reminder of the brutality of the world. "We see the dark side of life," Erin Worrell said to me more than once. The horrific news items people flinch away from is their daily reality; society deputizes them to deal with that for us.

Nevertheless, every forensic pathologist and death investigator I spoke to insists that if it gets under your skin, you need to find another line of work. "That may be someone else's loved one, but for me that's evidence," insists Chris Meditz, another investigator in Cleveland, and Worrell's sometime shift partner. "The only way I'm going to help everybody involved is by keeping that body as evidence and using that to get answers." The trick, they all agree, is to not take it home.

Still, when I asked Worrell and Meditz whether they've changed anything about their habits since taking their jobs, there was a long pause and then Worrell admitted that when both her daughters were infants, she insisted they sleep in their own rooms down the hall so she'd have to wake up fully and remain standing during night feedings—after seeing so many babies die from co-sleeping or accidental suffocation when a parent fell asleep, she didn't want to take any chances. Liz Mooney avoided autopsying infants for a little while after returning from maternity leave. Todd Barr said he steers clear of local news because he doesn't want a preview of tomorrow's work.

Mostly, they stop expecting to understand or predict human behavior. They know intimately that understanding the world as being guided by a coherent and meaningful narrative isn't possible. "It's hard for human nature. You always want to rationalize why somebody would do something. But sometimes you can't," Worrell says. "We've all had scenes where you come back and you just can't explain it."

She told me about one case that shook her, even though her ability to see each case as an exciting opportunity to learn new things borders on the outrageous. There was an older man who had lost the use of his arms and legs, and he'd been neglected, stranded in his bed until he died after what she suspected had been prolonged torture. The man's wife and adult children, who were his caretakers, suggested blandly that he'd died of natural causes. Later, Worrell pulled his social worker's notes and found years of documented abuse. "I had to take probably a half an hour and sit outside and not do anything. I was just like, I can't—I just—felt so bad for that guy. But then at the same time, one of the greatest parts of our job is that I'm his voice. And I'm gonna MOTHERFUCK that family for doing that to him."

I paused her for a second to ask what that meant. "I see that and I'm like, Okay, I'm here for you. I'm gonna protect you. All those people that mistreated you and left you there to rot and die? Fuck them. We're gonna get 'em. Me and you, buddy." She sat back in her chair and smiled. "And I did. They all pleaded guilty, the whole family got charged. It was a homicide." (The man's wife and children pled guilty to charges relating to his death.)

This is the coping mechanism that seems most important to all the people I spoke to—an attitude that terrible, horrible, unspeakable, very bad things happen every day, but that someone needs to show up and deal with it and help. Not everyone can do that, but they can. They talk about their work like care work: the dead are just people who have lost the ability to speak for themselves, and an autopsy is a concluding story. Some don't need their last story told because it's already known, but others need to be opened, looked at, interpreted, and spoken for.

The fundamental challenge of their profession is Americans' aversion to death. In America more than in other parts of the world, death is feared, siloed, anesthetized, disguised, ignored, and banished from the living in a strenuous display of the death-aversion Foucault described. Most medical students aren't even offered forensic pathology as a career option. Out of 131 medical schools in the United States, only 37 have accreditation for forensic pathology training.

"It wasn't even an option in medical school. Pathology was barely even taught," Todd Barr told me. It took him thirteen years of practicing medicine after graduating school to land in forensics, because for years he never knew about it, and once he did he was worried about starting over, and in a much less lucrative specialty. Liz Mooney knew from the start that she wanted to go into forensics, but had to push hard for her program to offer training in it. She eventually started a forensics club herself, calling up local coroners' offices and arranging for med students to observe autopsies.

Both Barr and Mooney point to the fundamental problem: people are suspicious of those who voluntarily deal with the dead. "I think it's the gore, the dirtiness of it," says Mooney. Forensic pathologists are not there to help people "get better," which subverts the common expectation of a physician's task. Even among physicians, she says, there's stigma attached to forensic pathology, and the assumption is that because they don't deal with live patients they must have only a rudimentary understanding of clinical medicine. She's had primary-care physicians accuse her of not being "a real doctor." The field receives less research funding and support because of the assumption that those dollars would make more impact in disciplines that heal or help the living.

This logic lies behind the crushing budget shortages that many coroners' and medical examiners' offices report. "My clientele are silent," Glenn Wagner told me. "They don't pay taxes anymore, they don't vote, and when a county, or a state for that matter, is looking at priorities in terms of work and health care, and all the government functions are tied to local services, those priorities are oftentimes and appropriately focused on the living, not on the dead. And so this office will always be in a negative role in competing with public health or the DA or the sheriff's office."

This belies the fact that spending money on the dead is spending money on the living. In Cleveland, the medical examiner's office works with the DEA, the postal service, and law enforcement to identify connected overdoses and the supply chains that cause them. They routinely make suggestions to city planners when they spot an intersection prone to fatal car accidents.

This aspect of their work rarely sees the light of day. A pathologist I spoke to in Montgomery County, Ohio, pointed out that the only times he and his colleagues show up in the news are in items about how they're the highest-paid positions in local government, and the stories never mention important trials they testified before or public health stories they're behind. He sighed. "We could use an 'atta boy' now and then."

Gilson and his colleagues argue that we have yet to realize the ways our revulsion toward death hurts our corporeal health. Americans' unwillingness to prioritize how we deal with the dead (or our supposition that the story, or the parts of it that matter, stop with the heartbeat) may constitute a failure of moral imagination, but it absolutely fails to imagine the way the living and the dead remain connected, no matter how the living feel about it. The dead tell us how we're dying, how we're living, who among us gets a better shot than others at a whole and healthy life, and how we remain vulnerable to one another and to the vicissitudes of an unpredictable world. Our epidemics, the commonality of our despair, our continual mistakes, the progress we have yet to make, the wrongs we have yet to correct—all these are mirrored back to us by the dead. No one likes to be reminded of these things, but they don't go away just because the bodies do.

Sitting at my dining table reading the other day, I reached up absentmindedly to pull on my hair, which was frizzy and bothering me. I tugged on the hair at the crown of my head, where my ponytail is, and felt distractedly that usual feeling, rarely registered, of scalp sliding forward and back on my skull. Not too far, just the amount it's supposed to, but back and forth, slipping.

Immediately, I saw the scalp on the autopsy table. My scalp stays in place when I tug on my ponytail only because the rest of my skin is here, one piece, insisting on its wholeness. It has its own limits, it regulates itself. When you violate that, we come apart like leather coin purses.

Is this what I wanted? To feel my own fragility, my own thing-ness, much more acutely than before? It's a morbid consequence of spending a lot of time around the dead, but if I am more careful crossing streets now, it's because it seems ludicrous and ungrateful to be cavalier once you've seen with your own eyes how easy it is to die. It may also be morbid that I think often about the people I came to know in their deaths with an intimacy I have with almost no one else—the inside of their skin, their unknown heart defects, what they kept in their bedrooms, their hidden vices, the things about their bodies they never told anyone, or never knew. People are so naked in death, naked in every way, their genitals so exposed on the table, their bodies thrown open for investigation like doors on an abandoned house.

It's a disquieting message with which to return from their world: no matter where society situates the cemetery, there is no them and us. We're just vulnerable. Inasmuch as I had bought into the delusion that by denying death we can escape it, I lost that thread of assurance. I did—as Foucault predicted of the atheist—come away with a stronger sense of the sanctity of the body as a "trace of our existence in the world and in language," though it seems false to suggest this is the only trace.

Still, it comforts me to know that once the autopsy is over, they sew you back together. They load your organs back into your chest cavity, gather your rib cage, and restitch the long slit from your chest to your pelvis with strong thread. They refit the top of your skull and tug your face and scalp back over it. They're careful, and make sure that once you are bathed and dressed, no one will be able to see your new seams. It's impossible to truly repair a body from an autopsy, but it is possible to restore the illusion of its wholeness. They place the paper bag of your belongings back on your belly. If they removed your wedding ring, they replace it. They call whoever it is who'll be coming for you, the person who knows your name, and tell them that you're ready.

When I was in Cleveland, I noticed that at the end of the afternoon meeting, as a parting salvo, Gilson always says the same thing. There was so much to take in that it took me a few days before I really heard it, and it wasn't until I caught Worrell and Meditz repeating it to each other in between their jokes and phone calls that I understood the phrase is like a mantra for the building. Instead of wishing his colleagues good night, Gilson puts one hand on the table, smiles, and commands them: "Celebrate the day."

Leaving the office every night, I'd get breathless rushes of reality. I'm here driving down the street in the dark. Cyndi Lauper is on the radio. Wow, I got to eat french fries tonight. Think of all the meals I've ever had. Think of all the times I've made it safely to bed at night. And woken up safely in the morning. Mixed in was sharp grief and powerful rage, flashes of the babies, or sisters, or grandfathers I'd seen on the autopsy table. For weeks and months, I'd get these rushes every few hours, like sine rhythms: I'm here. I'm here.

It reminded me of a poem that I've always loved but maybe not always understood—one Marie Howe addressed to her brother, Johnny, who died of AIDS when he was twenty-eight. With longing and exasperation, she describes to him the stupid practical business of the everyday: Drano, crusty dishes, spilling coffee. "This is what the living do," she writes, all these absurd, uncomfortable, banal things. "This is it. / Parking . . . What you called that yearning. / What you finally gave up."

But then, she writes,

there are moments, walking, when I catch a glimpse of myself in
*   the window glass,*
. . . and I'm gripped by a cherishing so deep
for my own blowing hair, chapped face, and unbuttoned coat that
*   I'm speechless:*
I am living. I remember you.

What feels so gratifyingly correct about this poem is that it acknowledges the way that shocks of your own aliveness come with a trace of elegy—for the future you who will no longer need a coat, but also for someone whose absence is as immediate and vital as your own presence.

Worrell and Meditz like to claim that the death investigators are the most high-spirited, grateful people in the building, and I noticed that they were also the ones who appeared never to forget someone who'd passed through the morgue. They were always saying, "Oh, I remember him," even about cases they hadn't personally attended. "Him? I remember him." They're not always reverent about it, but there's a specificity with which the people in this line of work, at their best, are always in a state of address: I am living; I remember you.

SOON THIS SPACE WILL BE TOO SMALL

From time to time you'll hear a writer suggest that we are all cursed, like Kierkegaard, to tell the same story over and over forever. Maggie Nelson suggests, less morosely, that we may "undergo the same realizations, write the same notes in the margin, return to the same themes in one's work, relearn the same emotional truths" not because we're cursed or stuck but because in fact "such revisitations constitute a life." She calls it, paraphrasing the psychoanalyst Donald Winnicott, "ordinary devotion."

Even if we are not all fated to circle a single story for our whole lives, perhaps we are obliged to follow a single thought all the way until we have finished it. Thoughts can take years. Lately I have been listening to a recording made by the song-writer Lhasa de Sela shortly before she died, at age thirty-seven, of breast cancer. When you talk about Lhasa in a room of musicians everyone gets sad because there is a common understanding that she was special, one of those people with a fingertip pressed to the universal pulse. When you hear her voice you can tell. It sounds like a coyote in the dark, a reed threaded down a long pipe.

In the recording, Lhasa is telling a story about her father, who is, she reports, a philosophical man. "Each idea that he has, its orbit takes several years to go around," she says. "And when he's really gone all the way through, then he has a new idea." These days, Lhasa says, her father has a new idea:

> His idea is that when we are conceived we appear in our mother's womb like a little tiny light, suspended in immense space. There's no sound. It's completely dark. And time doesn't seem to exist. It's like an ocean of darkness. . . . As we grow, slowly we begin to feel things and touch things, and touch the walls of our world that we're in. Then we begin to hear sounds and feel shocks that come to us from the outside, and as we get bigger and bigger, the distance between ourselves and that other outside world becomes smaller and smaller, and this world that we are inside that seemed so huge in the beginning and so infinitely welcoming, has become very uncomfortable. And we are obliged to be born.

Birth, her father suggests, is so chaotic and violent that we think it must be dying, the end of everything, and we are surprised to find ourselves delivered into a new world, so vast and incomprehensible that once again we are infinitely small and time is infinitely long. Again, we grow. We learn to touch the contours of the world that we're in.

This experience itself is circular. As we move through life, she says, we hear sounds and feel shocks that come from yet another world. Nearby, there is some other way of being we cannot yet imagine. And that other world is near, is with us, our whole lives long, sometimes faintly audible, as if something is happening just on the other side of a very, very thin wall. We can forget about it for a long time, and then it comes again.

BACKWARD MIRACLE

With respect to skin, wounds heal from the inside out and from the edges inward. This is dependable, though the exact process and speed of skin's resilience is less so because skin is as unique as the person inside it. A smoker in her fifties heals a cut more slowly than a teenage athlete; they both heal slower than a toddler; deep or jagged cuts take longer, and so on. These variables considered in combination allow you to approximate what's called "the algorithm of healing."

Still, there's normal healing. Take a wound gotten on a Tuesday morning while slicing an avocado. I was cupping a rounded half in my right hand, nosing the seed out with the tip of a serrated knife, when the seed came loose and rolled over like an eye in a socket, sending the knife down through the flesh and skin of the avocado and through the crook between my second and third fingers. It sawed straight to the joint where the metacarpal meets the knuckle, and suddenly I was in a crouch, panting lightly, spattering blood all over the kitchen floor and the countertop and—I'd learn later when the nurses wiped me off—my legs and face.

What is supposed to happen happened: the bleeding stopped, helped along by pressure and constricted blood vessels, and platelets flooded the wound and clotted. The doctor sewed eight crooked stitches to close the gap in my hand, and the healing began from the inside. Macrophages appeared to detect bacteria. Fibroblasts pumped the area with collagen, which connects tissues, and the skin began to knit itself together. There are names for what binds us: cytokines, arachidonic derivatives, leukotrienes, interferons, neutrophils. The body constructs an extracellular matrix, the scaffold upon which platelets, collagen, and endothelial progenitors begin to construct new blood vessels, granulated tissue, a new skin. It takes three to six weeks for the body to fully "bridge" a deep cut.

Ten days later, the doctor snipped and pulled her black wire stitches, wiped off a few crusts of blood, and introduced to me a new scar. "The nerves will grow back over the course of a year or two," she said when I told her my finger was numb. "A severed nerve has to send out networks of new cells across the wound, grasping around in the tissue until two find each other and can rebuild the connection." I should get used to the mark, though, she told me. The scar is the conclusive effect of healing.

The first ritualized tattoos we know of were traced on the bodies of women. The women were Egyptian, and they marked themselves with long strings of dots laid out in patterns to look like lines or diamonds. They tattooed their stomachs, their thighs, and their breasts, the ebbing and flowing skin of womanhood and motherhood. It is thought that the tattoos were for protection: they were positioned so that when the skin of the stomach swelled during pregnancy, the tattoos would stretch to resemble the nets of beads ritually laid over the bodies of the dead for protection in the afterlife. This protection written into the skin would cover a pregnancy; some of the women were found with the deity Bes, guardian of women in labor, inked on their inner thighs.

Humans throughout history have demonstrated the itch to ritually open skin and leave marks. According to Jane Caplan in her history of the tattoo in the West, *Written on the Body*, almost every human culture throughout time has tattooed. Straight down the list of civilizations: Nubians, Scythians, Thracians, Berbers, the Tayal, the Yoruba, pre-Columbian Mesoamericans. A group of women buried in Kubban around 2000 B.C. were found with blue tattoos, some matching the belly strings of the Egyptian women. A woman's body was found in a tomb in Altai covered with designs of mythical animals. In parts of the Solomon Islands, women used obsidian to tattoo one another with the forms of frigate birds. In Papua New Guinea, people used a sharpened rake punted into the skin with a sort of mallet. In Japan, they used bamboo rods. In Samoa—where it is said that two women, Taema and Tilafaiga, introduced the practice—traditional tattooing ceremonies were done with bone combs, boar tusks, and turtle shell. Maoris would slice the skin with a knife and then rub the wound over and over with a piece of greenstone or animal bone dipped in ink. In Rome, where they tattooed slaves with words like TAX PAID or STOP ME, I'M A RUNAWAY, the ink was made from gall and vitriol. They called tattoos stigmata.

In America, nearly a third of us have done it—half, if you limit the data set to people under forty. We put simple black lines on our skin, words, watercolor. We love arrows and clocks, compasses and feathers, dreamcatchers, Saturn, sound waves of the voices of people we love, punctuation marks and geometry of every variety. Names, dates, lyrics, misattributed inspirational quotes, Disney princesses, elaborate cephalopods. Cherry blossoms, crashing waves and shells, all kinds of phoenixes rising—from ashes, from crotches—panthers, the bodies of women, dragons, scorpions, signs of the Zodiac, every possible part of the tarot, trees, spiders, peace symbols, infinity symbols, rosary beads, innumerable skulls (eating roses, wearing top hats), Chinese characters, Japanese characters, Greek characters, Cyrillic characters. Crosses, wings, nods to the Gothic, and—always—faces of the dead: fathers, mothers, babies, the Virgin Mary, the Virgin Mary with half her face melting down toward her modest collar.

Many of us are not sure why we do this, or what accounts for the fact that tattooing, which was inadmissible in polite society sixty years ago, has mainstreamed so quickly. Until recently, the tattoo required an encounter with death, the risk of infection, the body pierced and breakable. Mortality was the ritual's subtext, not just because it lingered as a possible outcome but because the inscription's "permanence" is undermined by its canvas.

The verse of a traditional Samoan tattoo artist's song: *Your*

necklace may break, the fau tree may burst, but my tattooing is
indestructible. It is an everlasting gem that you will take into your
grave.

Indestructible—until the grave. This tension is still present
in modern tattooing, even though death by infection is no longer a serious concern. The other day, on an airplane, I sat next
to a man with a high and tight haircut and colorless lips, who
read with perfect stillness and beautiful posture as we jolted
our way through savage turbulence. On his forearm, tilted up
toward his face, were the words EVERYONE DIES.

That was maybe a little on the nose, but generally, by re-
minding us that we have bodies that will die, tattoos—like
anything that exposes what is inside us to what's outside—
recall people to moments of visceral contact with aliveness,
the fierce pumping glut of blood, the clench and unclench of
muscles waiting underneath our skin at all times, the pulpy
engine. Like most rituals of ecstasy and violence, ritual scarification historically signaled an audience with something divine,
a communion with the eternal regions of the self that can't be
reduced to flesh, or marked, or broken.

Among the Mohave, who lived for centuries in the valley
separating what would become California and Arizona, the
women were given tattoos to ensure their place in the afterlife.
They were voluntary—the Mohave never forced one another
to be tattooed—but most women got them. The inscriptions
were a mark of permanent spiritual belonging: when the bearer
arrived in the afterlife, her ancestors would recognize her as one
of their own by the lines on her chin, and welcome her. Even
after death, she could be known by what marked her.

———————

The first time I considered getting a tattoo, I was twenty-two years old. I was fresh out of college and waiting tables at a Spanish restaurant in SoHo. In the changing room at work, I was talking with my friend Chris, a beautiful, thin, faun-like man with giant eyes and a sharp chin, while he removed his street clothes and put on our branded work shirts. I spotted on his shoulder blade a line of black script that looked unusual. When I asked him about it, he said it was Michelangelo Buonarroti's handwriting. "I saw the angel in the marble and I carved until I set him free," he translated for me. I was smitten.

"It would be a line of text," I told my boyfriend at the time, "following the arc of a rib on the left side."

I liked the idea that it would be somewhere intimate but not overtly sexual, where few people would ever see it. Just a few words that I would need always, though it was the notion that appealed to me more than any particular phrase. I didn't know which words were important enough yet.

"Hot," my boyfriend said approvingly, rummaging for a sweater in the closet. "But you'll never do it." This irritated me. How did he know what I would or wouldn't do? But he was unmoved when I protested.

"I know you," he said, shrugging. "You'll never go through with it."

At the time, I thought I would marry him, so I accepted what he said. It seemed possible that he could see things about me that I couldn't see.

———

When, years later, I met you, you were dressed like the ghost of June Carter Cash. We were at a "Dead Poets" Halloween party thrown by some writer friends of mine, and everyone had been instructed to dress up as their favorite dead poet and bring a poem to perform in character. There was a Sappho, a Thoreau, a Robert Lowell, a John Berryman, an Anne Sexton, several Beats, and two Sylvia Plaths. I went with a friend who'd snapped up Elizabeth Bishop, and after some minor dithering I went as Adrienne Rich, which meant that I dressed in my own clothes.

I don't really remember meeting you as June. I was caught up with friends, I was in love with another woman. I vaguely recall a mutual friend waving me over to the corner for an introduction, and shaking hands with a tall woman wearing a braid. You are beautiful, but I don't remember your face from that night.

You remember meeting me more clearly, remember seeing me sitting up on a ledge with Elizabeth Bishop and Emily Dickinson. "I knew you were gay," you said years later, once we were together. "You had a gay face."

I was startled. "What does that mean?"

You shrugged, grinning your provocative grin. "I don't know, you just do. You have a gay face."

We repeat this conversation from time to time whenever you identify someone else who is ostensibly straight but about whom you have a feeling.

"But what are you seeing in the face that makes you say it's gay," I want to know.

"I don't know," you say, laughing. "But I know it when I see it."

"Which features? What about them?"

"The whole thing."

You are not helpful, mostly because you're joking and I'm serious.

The first time you said this, I went and looked again at the pictures from the Dead Poets night. My hair was long then, and I was wearing a blazer and dangling earrings. I look younger, maybe, and flushed and happy, but if anything, I think I look straight. I often look at pictures of myself from around that time, to see if I can see what you saw. I'm intrigued by the idea that queerness might be traceable in a face, that features can give away secrets you've kept even from yourself.

It is not novel to suggest that the skin is like a paper or a canvas, a surface to be interpreted, and that by extension tattoos can be "read" like text. Tattooed bodies are "moving frescoes," wrote Catherine Grognard, and the insignia inscribed on them are signs of a meaning that lies underneath. Tattoos, like poems, are "pointers or indications that tell us what we are searching for lies farther on," as Octavio Paz wrote. "The pilgrimage by way of the canvas or body tattooed with signs leads to an image that, as it vanishes, opens doors to us."

The first time I slept with the woman I loved before you, she started saying, "You're gay! Oh my god, you're gay," and she wouldn't stop. She seemed so shocked. We'd known each other for many years, and in that time she'd gotten to know me decently well, and it was as if she were having an epiphany about some essential quality she'd missed. I'd dated the same handsome, square-jawed man for five of those years. I had identified as straight without giving much thought to the way I sometimes pined for women, and as far as I was concerned in that moment, I still was, mostly. I was straight and in love with her.

Oh my god, you're gay. You're gay. Her eyes were so wide. If I recall correctly, I laughed and told her to shut up. I shoved something in her mouth. We started seeing each other.

Life is marked by these rapid and unanticipated moments of reversal. You believe in God, and then you do not, or vice versa; you feel safe until you do not; you are well until you are not; you are humming along vaguely bored by your life and then you're in love and everything, even you, looks different.

A few problematic paradigm shifts arise once you've experienced the before and after and then the after-that, once the cosmos has rearranged itself and then rearranged again and then disintegrated and reassembled, never with your permission. It makes you mistrust that upper-level, externally imposed certainty so easily accessed by religious converts, and then it makes you crave it. It made me want to get a tattoo. What else but total self-driven certainty could prompt a person to inscribe something into their skin? I wanted to feel beatifically sure about something. I took to drawing designs on myself in black ink.

Often, what I drew were dots in strange patterns, or stark,

abstract line configurations, but mostly I wrote sentences on myself. They were reliably someone else's, lines that I thought might be worth keeping. I thought of my body as a commonplace, material on which I could collage other minds and save them for future use. On my skin I could hold things without fear of losing them again. But I couldn't figure out which of these things, if any, would stand up to permanent ink. I was especially wary of tattooing words, which anyone could read. "To be marked is, again, to open oneself up to observation, to interpretation, to possession even," writes the scholar Jennifer Putzi. I stubbornly wanted to remain illegible to everyone except myself.

The first American white woman with tattoos was Olive Oatman, also known as Olivino Oach, or Ali, or Aliútman, or Spantsa. She was born Olive, one of seven children in a family of Brewsterites, a sect of Mormons who followed eleven-year-old James Colin Brewster, who prophesied that believers would receive their inheritances in the valleys of the Gila and Colorado Rivers in Arizona. In 1850, Olive's father, Roys, sold his farm in Illinois, loaded his seven children into a covered wagon, and joined Brewster on the journey west in search of heaven on earth.

Many months later, with fewer than two hundred miles to go, the family found themselves on Cooke's Wagon Road, standing on top of a mesa looking out over the Gila River. They were racing starvation through the desert: black lava rocks, ocotillo plants, bloody-tipped and spiky, bursting twenty feet up over the packed earth; legions of saguaro standing sentry.

The children spotted the Yavapai first, a small group coming on foot from the west. Olive counted nineteen. They had been warned about Apache in the area. White settlers had been violently annexing Apache land, and after the settlers put a bounty out on Apache scalps, Apache began attacking white emigrants in retribution. When the men approached and asked for food, Olive's father declined, pleading that his family was already starving. Olive's mother, nine months pregnant, retreated to the wagon with the youngest children, still toddlers. The Yavapai asked again, and so he gave them bread, and then they asked for more, and he refused, and then they clubbed the family to death.

"When I recovered my thoughts," Olive wrote many years later, "I thought I was probably dying. I knew that probably all the family had been murdered. . . . Occasionally a low, piteous moan would come from some one of the family as in a dying state." As the Yavapai searched the wagon, they tore apart the duvet bedding with a knife, sending the down feathers out on the wind, scattering off over the edge of the mesa and sticking in the blood.

Olive and her younger sister Mary Ann were taken as captives by the Yavapai until, a year later, a group of Mohave spotted them on a seasonal trading visit and traded for them. Olive and Mary Ann were adopted into the family of one of the festival chiefs, a man named Espaniole, and given a garden plot and seeds in Mohave Valley.

Within a few years, the girls were fluent in Mohave and had forgotten much of their English. They wore willow bark skirts and nothing else, painted their faces, and dyed their hair black with the gum of mesquite trees. As Mohave girls, they played with dice made out of cottonwood, ran races, climbed trees, and swam every day. They went by Espaniole's family name, Oach, and Olive became Olivino, or Ali. More often, she went by Spantsa, which meant something like "insatiable."

When they had been living with the Mohave for a few years, Olive later told, their Mohave mother, Aespaneo, came to the girls to tell them that Espaniole and two doctors were waiting in the yard. It was time for them to receive their tattoos.

This was their formal initiation and acceptance into the tribe, an acknowledgment that their souls had become permanently Mohave. With the chin markings, Olive would be recognized after death by her ancestors—not her birth mother and father, but her adopted ancestors, who would know her as one of their own and welcome her to the Land of the Dead. Margot Mifflin, one of the biographers who later wrote about Olive, points out that this moment of inscription was the moment Olive irrevocably passed out of the world she had come from. Not only did she reassign her soul's destination from a Mormon celestial kingdom to a Mohave Land of the Dead, she reassigned herself in life. There were no white women with tattoos, and certainly no Mormons. With a tattoo, she would no longer be what she had been.

Olive lay down in the grass, with her head in the lap of the doctor, while he slowly drew the designs on her chin with charcoal. "They pricked the skin in small regular rows on our chins with a very sharp stick," she wrote later, "until they bled freely. They then dipped these same sticks in the juice of a certain weed that grew on the banks of the river, and then in the powder of a blue stone that was to be found in low water." For hours, they repeated this gesture: prick, bleed, dip, rub.

Later, there would be confusion about whether she'd wanted this, but we know for sure that she lay still in the doctor's lap and took care with the scarring because her lines, when they healed, healed straight.

Mary Ann had been weaker than Olive from the start, and shortly after they were tattooed she succumbed to a famine that swept Mohave Valley. The accounts tell us that when Mary Ann died, Olive wailed like a Mohave, but when the tribal mourning rituals were over, Olive begged them not to burn the body. The chiefs balked—Mohave were cremated, never buried—but her begging was so desperate that they agreed. Olive buried Mary Ann in their garden under the hyacinth, like a Christian.

Rumors of a white woman living with the Mohave reached federal authorities at Fort Yuma, who sent an envoy to demand her return. A friend of Olive's named Musk Melon later recalled that Espaniole told the envoy, "I would like to raise this girl. We traveled far to buy her. We like her." But the men threatened to kill the whole tribe if Olive wasn't released. White men are hiding in the mountains, they told the tribe chiefs, and they will descend and kill all of you if the girl isn't returned.

Eventually, the Mohave relented. Olive would be traded back for two horses, and some blankets and beads. Witnesses said that when the deal was announced, Olive burst into tears. She was sent to Fort Yuma with an escort, holding a branch of the hyacinth in her hand.

She was sent to the home of Susan Thompson Parrish, one of the Brewsterite children who had traveled with the Oatmans. These are lines from Parrish's diary at the time:

Many years later
They found the girl
in her bark dress
seated
on the river bank
At the approach
of the white men
she buried herself
in the sand.

Olive's return provoked a media frenzy. Articles were run and flyers printed: FIVE YEARS AMONG WILD SAVAGES. A sculpture was done in her honor by Erastus Dow Palmer in 1858, called *The White Captive*, and audiences thronged to see it in New York. The sculpture is a girl, pubescent and distressed. She is naked and tied to a post with her nightgown. Her marble skin is white and unmarked. The girl is bound but still virginal, imperiled but untouched. *"The White Captive* relies on a belief that the classical body—closed and self-contained—can withstand any disruption or penetration, even if that body is nude and female," writes Jennifer Putzi.

Not so with Olive, who arrived back to Fort Yuma having forgotten most of her English, naked to the waist, with dyed dark hair, painted and tattooed on her arms and face. Susan Thompson Parrish described Olive in her diary as a "frightened, tatooed [*sic*] creature who was more savage than civilized, and who sought at every opportunity to flee back to her Indian husband and children." (Olive later denied that she had been married or borne children while with the Mohave.)

Olive was a national sensation. News stories assured the world that she had not been sexually defiled. A *Los Angeles Star* article described how people "rushed to see her and stare at her, with about as much a sense of feeling as they would to a show of wild animals." She was nineteen.

At the time, and until the mid-twentieth century, when tattooing hit mainstream Western culture, bodily adornment was a sign of extreme otherness within modern white society. There had been a few upper-class forays into tattooing in Europe (the Prince of Wales got one in 1860; Winston Churchill's mother had one), but the practice remained mostly the province of nonwhite cultures like the Maori or Samoans, or of outsiders, like sailors and prisoners. Among Europeans and Americans, tattoos coded racial or class taint.

When Captain Cook returned from Polynesia and imported the word "tattoo," which meant to puncture, or to write, he imported another word to English: "taboo." It was also a Samoan word that was translated to Cook as both sacred and forbidden, set apart, too holy or too profane to be touched.

Olive's body had become the latter by dint of the former. She was no longer quite white, but neither was she Mohave. Her in-betweenness was written on her face; some part of the Mohave had penetrated her, and everyone could see.

So she wrote a book. Or she allowed an enterprising minister named Royal Stratton to write her memoirs, a document that scholars have agreed alters facts, contradicts Olive's first accounts of her time with the Mohave, and recasts her, falsely, as a slave. The book was first issued in 1857, and it sold out in three weeks—captivity literature by white women was already a bestselling genre. By 1860, it had sold twenty-six thousand copies. For six years, she took her face on tour with the book, and recanted what she had first said upon returning: that she had been at home with the Mohave, that she had been well treated, that she had loved Mohave Valley.

Olive became the first tattooed woman to exhibit herself for profit, a violation of white America's strictures for women—who were not generally allowed to lecture publicly— that she was permitted because she was no longer quite white, and no longer, in some abstract sense, a normal woman.

No one knows whether she believed what she said on tour. Margot Mifflin suggests that Oatman displayed herself as a victim and resentful former captive in part to ensure herself against the suspicion and judgment that came from having been a woman called "insatiable" who lived bare-breasted in the wilds of Arizona. She couldn't pretend that she hadn't been "tainted":

the evidence was on her face. She also needed the money that lecturing earned her, Mifflin points out—what man would marry her now?

When she lectured, she would draw people's attention to the lines on her face, presenting her body as the center of an unfolding American drama that "brings into view the rudest barbarism & the highest civilization." She was bewitching: "The audience listened with breathless interest, and all were deeply affected," wrote a reporter for *The New York Times*. Throngs of people came to see her and hear "her pathetic story, surpassing in interest the most thrilling romance," as the *Rochester Daily Union and Advertiser* reported. They watched her as one might watch a feather that had been transformed to a tiger and then back again. She stood before them on the podium claiming that she was and was not the same as before, that she was both herself and not.

A disproportionate number of the tattoos ever given marked chimeric transformations, moments where the self breaks open and becomes some other self, the unsustainable liminal state. They provoke or safeguard against crisis: Egyptian women in labor, Maori boys in their rites of passage, Mohave being delivered from death to afterlife. Some of the earliest tattoos were images of chimeras, impossible, imaginary hybrid animals. The Pazyryks, whose mummified bodies were found in Siberia, were delivered to their burial chambers covered in them: fish turning into monsters, a creature with horns turned into flowers, conjoined rams, a deer whose back legs pointed toward the sky. In *The Archaeology of Death and Burial*, Michael Parker Pearson writes that these creatures "may be perceived not only as 'imaginary' but also as liminal 'betwixt and between' creatures of danger, power, violence."

These creatures are magical and powerful, given access to many worlds, but think about their bodies: patchwork constructions reassembled from pieces of whole animals that have been torn from themselves. One can't come without the other—that's the rule of the hybrid—but disarticulation also involves wounding. *Nepantla*, Gloria Anzaldúa wrote, is both generative and chaotic and painful; it involves the "anguish" of "crossing a series of cruz calles, junctures, and thresholds, some leading to a different way . . . and others to the creation of a new world."

When I fell in love with a woman for the first time, I felt like I had already been thrust across one too many thresholds in my life. I had found God and lost God; I had seen my mind grow ill and foreign to me, and watched it return; I had imagined one spouse and one career, and then begun again. I wasn't prepared for another experience of radical change or of disorienting liminality. I didn't even anticipate that getting into it, I just did it because there wasn't much choice involved: I loved her.

As I did, the world started to change around me. I became invisible to men, or so it felt—I abruptly stopped getting hit on in public places. I started noticing women in public spaces who were queer, and they started noticing me. It was like gaining a sixth sense. I felt looser in my body. I started telling the people who had known me for a long time that I was in love with a woman and noticing the way they were stunned, the way they acted as if I were revealing myself to be an essentially different person than the one they'd known. I didn't think it was that big a leap, mostly because to me it felt so natural, but met with this news, people suddenly looked at me as if I were a stranger to them, or as if they were realizing I had been a stranger all along. I kept having to tell the people to whom I'd been the closest, "It is me, still. I am exactly who I was yesterday." It was true and it wasn't.

Being with a woman felt freeing and joyful and somehow important—but dating men was an easier, more habitual mode of being for me. Except that it wasn't. "Both," I told an old friend who was trying to wrap her head around it. "I love both."

She looked at me patiently. "But eventually you have to choose."

My notes from that time tell me that at one point I considered a tattoo that read:

19. Accept loss forever.
20. Believe in the holy contour of life.

Of course I didn't get it. Even at my most melodramatic, I understood that one never lives down a Kerouac tattoo.

There's a picture of Olive sitting on my desk, one taken after she returned east from the desert. In this photo, she is twenty-three. She is back in Protestant America, and she is standing in a heavy silk gown with a bell-shaped crinoline and pagoda sleeves. Her collar is tatted and her hair is parted down the center, twisted back behind each ear, and curled carefully so the waxed ringlets fall in precise one-inch coils. She has placed one hand on the back of an ornate Louis XVI–style carved chair. The tattoos on her chin match the embroidery on her voluptuous sleeves and hem: like a musical staff bisected with diagonal slashes. The effect is strange, and judging by the set of her jaw and the directness of her gaze, she knows.

Not long after her book tour, she married a man named Fairchild who tried to buy up all the copies of her book and burn them. She lived to be sixty-five, and for the rest of her life she appeared in public under veils. Still, she wrote in letters to friends that she was happy with him and the daughter they adopted and named Mamie.

In her biography of Olive Oatman, Mifflin suggests that we're still writing and thinking about Oatman because she is "a poster girl for our inherently split and perpetually multiplying national identity."

Oatman stood at the crossroads of history when the West was stolen . . . Oatman's story reflects the crossed boundaries and trampled frontiers that marked this transaction. She survived the botched pursuit of the American Dream, arrived at a geographical and utopian terminus—California—where, as Joan Didion famously put it, "we ran out of continent." Then, reborn as a white Mohave, she turned around and went east again. Her blue tattoo became a poignant, permanent, ethnic marker, invoking both the cultural imprint of her Mohave past and the lingering scars of westward expansion.

Olive's story serves as a parable for the violence of the American project, the brutal insistence on dividing the world between "white" and "other," between "civilization" and "savagery," that underpinned this country's formation. It's not only violent to police these kinds of binaries—it's impossible. Olive was evidence of that impossibility, an artifact of that upheaval. Her face was the face of "a white woman of color, a foreigner in her own country . . . No American immigrants or captives have worn their hybrid identities so publicly."

One thing to appreciate about tattoos is that they're a violence you can undertake and survive. "The body can be bled, carved, and inscribed, and yet it lives on after the inscription: reassuringly the same and yet different," wrote Lucien Taylor. This is the mundane miracle Olive offers, the reason people still write her story: the visibility of her wounds inflicted by the power of fate and history, and the implacability of her scarred survival.

The version of her that survives is the woman staring out of this photograph with a trace of defiance. There's a real privacy to this photo, even as her bothness is written right there on her face. Oatman's life has been the subject of movies, written into short stories, elegized and re-elegized by newspapers, and always it is this photo they use: this calm, healed, marked woman.

Let's make this faster. For four years, years in which I went to church and then stopped going to church, fell in love and had my heart broken, moved three times and came out as what the ex-boyfriend who used to say my face looked "vaguely panethnic" might call "vaguely pansexual," I looked for a tattoo. I watched other people who were stuck in between one world and the next. I jotted down words and threw them away. I waited to see what would stick. Mostly, I wrote what I couldn't tattoo. These were, probably not coincidentally, the years in which I began to write in earnest, testing out ideas, places, people, lines that would be enduring enough to commit to paper, if not skin.

There was no epiphany, no angel crashing through the ceiling, no reconciliation with any ex, no one moment when I realized I wanted to stop going to church, no one day when my taste came back. I discovered, slowly, that I didn't want to "pass"—as white or Mexican, religious or agnostic, gay or straight, or anything else. "Passing" suggests movement, as if the passer moves physically back and forth between places, rather than just carrying both places, or all places, inside them at once. The issue with thinking about "passing" the usual way is that it suggests that fixed meaning or self is possible, that identity comes in tidy categories, that sex is legible, that faith is a binary state, and that any of these things can be made separate from the others. If the human body is made grotesque by a tattoo, as the theorist Mary Russo wrote, "open, protruding, irregular, secreting, multiple, and changing," it is because we already are.

I ran across a passage from *Le ruban au cou d'Olympia*, by the French surrealist Michel Leiris, that I roughly translate this way:

Because he couldn't tattoo the whole surface of his skin with the contents of his mind, he decided—because it would be unthinkable to leave bare the parts of his body he couldn't reach—that he would confide to paper what he wanted known of himself. But, in spite of certain advantages this afforded (avoiding the delicate problems of layout, limited space, or making public certain things that propriety obliges one to keep private—and even having found something more durable than his body to carry the message), the solution seemed a poor substitute. Writing was indirect, projecting everything on a screen instead of giving it life, giving over his body, binding it to inscriptions and images more intimately than foam or lichen could cling to a rock. His words could never be so eloquent as his flesh, the organ of his life and vessel of his spirit, turned thus into a kind of damask. He might have become a book of incantations written upon the most natural incantation of all, full to bursting with meaning and defiant before death.

When I finally did it, I took the train down to Sunset Park in Brooklyn and walked along a narrow, cold park to the house of a girl who'd been recommended by a friend. She was just getting started doing tattoos out of her house, and would charge me only forty dollars, which sounded like a good idea at the time. I remember that she was about my age and that she invited me into her bedroom, which was large and bright, where her tattoo gun was set up at a little table in the corner. We sat down and drew three dots on my wrist in black marker, running straight across the watch line on the inside. I'd done it so many times myself, doodling, that it felt like completing a sentence.

"And see how the flesh grows back / across a wound, with a great vehemence," wrote the poet Jane Hirshfield:

> more strong
> than the simple, untested surface before.
> There's a name for it on horses,
> when it comes back darker and raised: proud flesh.

If the scar or the mark is the signpost of the way the world has written on you, opened you, the tattoo is the evidence of how you have written on yourself—how you have manipulated your body's mandate to heal.

The other day, I was watching a video of what appeared to be a woolly pair of bell-bottom pants pulling a giant gumdrop by a fibrous tether along a ridge, one knock-kneed step at a time. The gumdrop was jewel green, and as it was dragged, its sugar granules swirled and bunched like the skin on a horse's back. Its leader had the bloody pinkness of an umbilical cord. The tether appeared wet. Together they looked familiar, like characters from a dream half-remembered.

I showed it to you and you wrinkled your nose. "Is that a bug thing?"

According to the video's caption, the bell-bottoms were a myosin protein and the gumdrop a ball of endorphins, the ridge a live filament connecting two pieces of the parietal cortex. It wasn't so much a bug thing as a brain thing, a portrait of the microscopic cellular dramas that constitute our feelings.

"This is what happiness actually looks like," said the caption.

When I told you, you paused, readjusting your vision, and then frowned. "Why is nobody helping him?"

It's true that the bell-bottom protein did look like a little headless fellow and that his load looked Sisyphean. The video was looped in such a way that his walk appeared never-ending, which made his wobbly steadfastness in the face of nonarrival sort of poignant. This is what happiness actually looks like: a tiny gross hero carrying on.

You sometimes talk about these years I've been describing, the years before we got together, as your era of bricklaying. During that time, you had the sense that you needed to slowly, methodically exert yourself toward an unseen goal, as if you were laying bricks to build a house without knowing its floor plan. You found an apartment, scrubbed down all its walls, and filled it with straightforward wood furniture. You bought light curtains. You learned to stay with someone who was kind to you, which had not been your habit. This wasn't exactly happiness, but it was something related. It was what you had to do first.

I'd never really thought of happiness as something with prerequisite architecture, something that demanded a house before it would come to stay. Instead, my instinct had always been to treat it more like a flare, rising spontaneously and dramatically in the dark, lighting the path. In this sense I used happiness as a barometer of nourishment and goodness, the soul equivalent of the feeling you get when eating a burger and realizing, in the intense, unexpected relief of meat, that you've been anemic.

Anyone with a background in theology or ethics or psychology or really anything to do with human behavior will tell you that this is a terrible idea, popular adages about "following your bliss" notwithstanding. Happiness alone is a faulty guide to making a life because it doesn't readily discriminate between short-term delight and long-term wellness.

Nevertheless, for several years, while you were laying bricks, I was looking for happiness flares and stumbling after them. For a few years I gave over my major decisions to a series of powerful intuitions, looking for the algorithm of healing, the rules of joy. I have plenty of marks from that time, but none more public than the three dots on my wrist. Ironically, the girl who gave me that first tattoo made a mistake. She was still getting to know her gun, and she drove the ink in too deep and fast. Immediately, a haze of blue began to seep through the deep tissue of my wrist, as if she'd hit a vein. Don't worry, she said, it's just some extra ink bleeding off, it'll go away in a few days. It never did. If the years between then and now are any indication, I'll have that washy blue under the dots on my wrist forever. It's okay.

When we met, that tattoo was healed and I was already thinking about a second one. I was drawn to you not so much by capricious emotional weather, as most of my decisions were seeming to me just then, but by some steadier gravity, the way the moon follows the sun. The first week we were together you showed me, unprompted, a poem by Kay Ryan that I'd never seen before:

Every once in a while
we need a
backward miracle
that will strip language,
make it hold *for*
a minute: just the
vessel with the
wine in it—
a sacramental
refusal to multiply,
reclaiming the
single loaf
and the single
fish thereby.

I wrote it down and pinned it to your mirror, where it still is.

This was my first indication that some joy can be steady even as it admits shifts and change, that a single choice can be as capacious and tidal as a person. That the body heals when it does. That sometimes language can just hold what is.

Our happiness together was brilliant: One summer morning, we decided to walk from Flatbush all the way to the ocean and stopped midway to buy lunch. We bought a giant ball of mozzarella, wet and still warm, and took it to the frail wooden bench outside the shop. You tore it apart ceremonially, handing me shreds one at a time, and we ate it, not talking much. An old man walked by and, seeing the look on our faces, cried, "AH! AMOR!" Later, you took me to the Mojave Desert, full of ocotillo and sage, where the dunes migrate in the wind and the sunrises are a purple that is also orange, and hiked me to the highest spine of the tallest dune.

Every once in a while you ask me what my three dots mean, even though you know I won't tell you. That was my deal with myself—that mark would be only mine. It's a code only I could read: no matter what new world I landed in, wherever or whatever or whoever that might be, I would be recognizable to myself.

This I can tell you: When I came to your apartment for the first time, I recognized it. I knew, without knowing how, that I would never leave. These were the bricks you had been laying without knowing it; this was the path my flares had been lighting. It was the beginning of a wobbly and joyful and occasionally gross carrying on, learning to come home to you, marked and myself.

NOTES AND WORKS CONSULTED

ATTUNEMENT

Samuel Beckett, *Waiting for Godot*

Michel Foucault, "Of Other Spaces: On Heterotopias and Utopias"

Søren Kierkegaard, *Fear and Trembling*

Tony Kushner, *Angels in America*

Maggie Nelson, *The Argonauts*

Rainer Maria Rilke, *Duino Elegies*

Lhasa de Sela, "Soon This Space Will Be Too Small"

Simone Weil, "The Love of God and Affliction"

Christian Wiman, "I Will Love You in the Summertime," *The American Scholar*

THIN PLACES

Eula Biss, *On Immunity*

Lennard J. Davis, *Obsession: A History*

Sigmund Freud, "Notes Upon a Case of Obsessional Neurosis"

Sigmund Freud, "The Uncanny"

Ann Hamilton, "Making—And the Spaces We Share" (interview with Krista Tippett)

Ian Jakes, *Theoretical Approaches to Obsessive-Compulsive Disorder*

Heidi Julavits, "Diagnose This," *Harper's Magazine*

Toni Morrison, *Beloved*

William Shakespeare, *Romeo and Juliet*

Susan Sontag, *Illness as Metaphor*
Mark Strand, "In Memory of Joseph Brodsky"

JESUS RAVES

A note about this essay: "Jesus Raves" was reported and written in 2013 and 2014. In revising the piece for this book, I chose not to change certain outdated facts to preserve the narrative integrity of the story as it was originally written. Naturally, the circumstances of some characters have changed as time has passed—Jessi and Parker no longer live in New York City or work for Liberty Church; Liberty Church itself has expanded and shifted beyond the portrait that is sketched here. To my knowledge, Liberty no longer holds pop-up churches in Montauk or makes a point of proselytizing in nightclubs. Some of the names in this essay have been changed.

THE BIG EMPTY

The complete works of Ann Hamilton
Gaston Bachelard, *The Poetics of Space*
Amy Benson, "Other Places," *New England Review*
Roberta Smith, "Ann Hamilton at the Park Avenue Armory," *The New York Times*
Simone Weil, *Gravity and Grace*

GOOD KARMA

The Lone Pine Museum of Western Film History
Abby Aguirre, "Where *Chinatown* Began," *Vogue*
Jean Baudrillard, *America*
Mike McPhate, "The Surprise Reincarnation of Owens Lake," *California Sun*
Karen Piper, "Dreams, Dust and Birds," *Places*

HABITUS

Nancy Acevedo-Gil, "Toward a Critical Race Nepantlera Methodology," *Cultural Studies, Critical Methodologies*
Ana M. Alonso, "Borders, Sovereignty, and Racialization," *A Companion to Latin American Anthropology*
Gloria Anzaldúa, *Borderlands/La Frontera*
Greg Grandin, *The End of the Myth*
AnaLouise Keating, "From Borderlands and New Mestizas to Nepantlas and Nepantleras," *Human Architecture*

NOTES AND WORKS CONSULTED

AnaLouise Keating and Gloria Gonzalez-Lopez, eds., *Bridging: How Gloria Anzaldúa's Life and Work Transformed Our Own*

Eithne Luibhéid, "Queer/Migration: An Unruly Body of Scholarship," *GLQ*

Valeria Luiselli, *Lost Children Archive*

Ed Morales, *Latinx*

Mariana Ortega, "The New *Mestiza* and *La Nepantlera*," *In-Between*

Emma Pérez, "Queering the Borderlands," *Frontiers*

Say Yes to the Dress

Sarah Smith, Nathan W. Swanson, and Banu Gökariksel, "Territories, Bodies and Borders," *Area*

Susan Sontag, "Notes on Camp"

Luís Alberto Urrea, *The House of Broken Angels*

Melissa Wright, "Maquiladora Mestizas and a Feminist Border Politics: Revising Anzaldúa," *Hypatia*

STITCHING

Tony Kushner, *Angels in America*

LoveTaza.com

SHAKERS

Archives of the Sabbathday Lake Shaker Village library

The Shaker Collection at the New York State Museum

Rima Sabina Aouf, "Shaker Style Is Back Again as Designers Celebrate 'The First Minimalists,'" *Dezeen*

Ken Burns, *The Shakers*

"'Let Us Labor': The Evolution of Shaker Dance," *Shaker Heritage Society*

Paul Rocheleau, *Shaker Built: The Form and Function of Shaker Architecture*

Mary Ruefle, *My Private Property*

The Wooster Group, *Early Shaker Spirituals: A Record Album Interpretation*

A THEORY OF IMMORTALITY

Eula Biss, *On Immunity*

THE OTHER CITY

Marie Howe, "What the Living Do"

Tony Kushner, *Angels in America*

Michel Foucault, "Of Other Spaces: On Heterotopias and Utopias"

SOON THIS SPACE WILL BE TOO SMALL

Maggie Nelson, *The Argonauts*
Lhasa de Sela, "Soon This Space Will Be Too Small"
D. S. Winnicott

BACKWARD MIRACLE

Jane Caplan, *Written on the Body*
Mark Doty, "Visitation"
Catherine Grognard and Claudio Lazi, *The Tattoo: Graffiti for the Soul*
Jane Hirshfield, "Proud Flesh"
Franz Kafka, "The Penal Colony"
Michel Leiris, *Le ruban au cou d'Olympia*
Frances E. Mascia-Lees, *Tattoo, Torture, Mutilation, and Adornment: The Denaturalization of the Body in Culture and Text*
Margot Mifflin, *The Blue Tattoo*
Margot Mifflin, *Bodies of Subversion: A Secret History of Women and Tattoo*
Maggie Nelson, *The Argonauts*
Amelia Osterud, *The Tattooed Lady: A History*
Jennifer Putzi, *Identifying Marks: Race, Gender, and the Marked Body in Nineteenth-Century America*
Margaret Rau, *The Ordeal of Olive Oatman*
John Rush, *Spiritual Tattoo: A Cultural History of Tattooing, Piercing, Scarification, Branding, and Implants*
Mary Russo, *The Grotesque*
Kay Ryan, "Backward Miracle"
George Saunders, introduction to Donald Antrim's *The Verificationist*
R. B. Stratton, *Captivity of the Oatman Girls*
Nikki Sullivan, *Tattooed Bodies: Subjectivity, Textuality, Ethics, and Pleasure*

ACKNOWLEDGMENTS

This book is for—and dedicated to, and made possible by—a number of kind souls without whom I'd have never been brave enough to write. Let me name them here.

First thanks go to Claudia Ballard for her kindness, patience, good humor, good advice, and unflagging belief in this book.

To Colin Dickerman, for bringing it so beautifully into the world.

To my teachers: Alex Ross, for setting me on the path; to Margo Jefferson, for fortification; to Amy Benson, for the arc of epiphany; to Kate Zambreno, for giving permission; to Phillip Lopate, for asking hard questions; to Hilton Als and Leslie Jamison, for being the first readers of this manuscript; and to Heidi Julavits and Dottie Lasky, for trusting me with your students.

To my editors, who are also my teachers: Dayna Tortorici, who gave me my first assignment—I'm so grateful. To Marco Roth, who insisted that I finish "Thin Places" when I tried to throw it away. Also to Carla Blumenkranz, Chad Harbach, and Keith Gessen, whose patience and sharp eyes shepherded me when I was learning.

To Sasha Weiss at *The New York Times Magazine*, Kit Rachlis at *The California Sunday Magazine*, Hayden Bennett at *The Believer*, Robert Wilson at *The American Scholar*.

To Amelia Stein, for teaching me to write by example.

To Fannie Bialek, Rebecca Taylor, Molly Borowitz, Jonathan Fetter-Vorm, Kent Szlauderbach, Chloe Angyal, my fellow travelers and kindred spirits.

To Kristin Dombek, for *Fear & Trembling*.

To Maud Doyle, Moeko Fujii, Heather Radke, Jessi Stevens, and Kay Zhang, for early editing and steady camaraderie.

To Suleika Jaouad, Jayson Greene, Melissa Febos, Tara Westover, Scott Frank, and Jon Batiste, for later reads and encouragement.

To Luc Rioual, for his friendship and the line edit of a lifetime.

To Hannah Kaplan, for her research assistance and excellent company.

It's sort of irregular to thank people with whom you have no actual relationship, but this book arose from conversations of the mind with a handful of writers whose work has made mine feel possible. Endless gratitude to Marie Howe, Mark Doty, Amy Fusselman, Mary Ruefle, Eula Biss, and Maggie Nelson.

To my family, for their unflagging support and trust, and especially to my mother, whose grace at the prospect of appearing in this book was a towering example of courage and love.

Finally, thank you, Lora-Faye, for Lhasa and for this life.

A NOTE ABOUT THE AUTHOR

Jordan Kisner's writing has appeared in *n+1*, *The New York Times Magazine*, *The Atlantic*, *GQ*, *The Guardian*, *The American Scholar*, *The California Sunday Magazine*, *The New Yorker*, *The New Republic*, *New York*, *Pop-Up Magazine*, and *Pitchfork*, among other publications. Her work has received a Pushcart Prize and was selected for *The Best American Essays 2016*. She teaches creative writing at Columbia University.